"This very moving book is . . . a step beyond the Jerry Kramer that all of us have known before."
—Rod McKuen

". . . I wasn't very knowledgeable about business, but I liked the excitement of it, just as I liked the excitement of football. Competition is the main thing in both fields, and if you don't enjoy competition—clean, hard competition, I mean—you're not going to be a huge success in either . . . And I've found, in meeting all kinds of people, that the ones who get to the top, as lawyers or doctors or singers or writers, are the ones who have a strong competitive instinct. I'm like that. I want to win, at poker, golf, and everything else."

JERRY KRAMER'S
FAREWELL TO FOOTBALL
Edited by DICK SCHAAP

---

with a Foreword by ROD McKUEN

A NATIONAL GENERAL COMPANY

JERRY KRAMER'S
FAREWELL TO FOOTBALL

*A Bantam Book / published by arrangement with
The World Publishing Company*

PRINTING HISTORY

*World Publishing Company edition published September 1969
Bantam edition published August 1970*

Photographs courtesy of Vernon J. Biever

Published simultaneously in the United States and Canada

PRINTED IN THE UNITED STATES OF AMERICA

FOR MY THREE CHILDREN,

DIANE, DANNY, AND ESPECIALLY TONY, my oldest,
who has been fighting a speech impediment since birth,
who knows the meaning of dedication and
of second effort, and who won't give up until he wins.

Contents

Foreword

Jerry Kramer: An Appreciation

YOU KNOW THAT he could break you in half. He proves that with a handshake. But for a man who has spent so many Sundays slamming down the field with destruction in his eye, Jerry Kramer is an incredibly gentle man.

Though he's spent more time taped up, hospitalized, or coaxing wounds to heal than he has playing football, though his physical scars are many, his mental scars are few, if any at all. Jerry plays hard, in football or in friendship; wrestling with his kids or the stock market, he plays to win.

For Jerry Kramer, *Farewell to Football* will be hard. I know because I'm one of those who attempted over the past year to talk him out of the game. Jerry's been in training for some time for a new kind of life—a life away from the made-up image of the dumb footballer. Though he's often as shy as he is big, he has about him a sense of excellence that will take him anywhere he wants to go.

Football loses someone very special in Jerry Kramer. I for one am glad. Even though I cheered him on the field, I always worried if that one unbroken finger would remain intact. I care about Jerry Kramer as a friend and as a man and I care enough to want to see his sense of excellence reach beyond the limits of the weekend goal posts.

This very moving book is more than another *Instant Replay*. It is a step beyond the Jerry Kramer that all of us have known before.

ROD McKUEN

New York City, May 1969

Editor's Note

THIS IS, ONCE again, Jerry Kramer's book, his thoughts, his impressions, his words. As in *Instant Replay*, it is his perception and his sensitivity that bring *Farewell to Football* to life.

This is not, in the normal sense, a sequel. *Farewell to Football* is not a diary. It is partly an autobiography, which means, in the case of Jerry Kramer, that it is partly a medical journal, a chronicle of his ailments. And *Farewell to Football* is partly a summation of one man's beliefs and one man's doubts, which means, in the case of Jerry Kramer, that it is totally honest, that he judges himself more severely than he judges anyone else.

The win-or-lose suspense of *Instant Replay* has been replaced by a different kind of suspense, a lingering, subjective suspense. *Farewell to Football* traces the development of a man, rather than the development of a season, and there is no pure statistical way to measure the success of a man. Jerry Kramer is only thirty-three, and most of his life lies ahead of him.

We gathered the material for *Farewell to Football* in much the same way that we assembled *Instant Replay*. After the 1968 season ended, during the weeks when Jerry Kramer reached his decision to retire from professional football, he and I sat, with a tape recorder between us, and explored for many hours and hundreds of thousands of words his memory and his emotions. He is a gifted storyteller, and he is, by now, totally at ease with the recorder. He finds it as sympathetic as an analyst, and considerably less expensive.

We discovered that, with this book, we could communicate in a special kind of shorthand. *Instant Replay* had, in a way, put me inside Jerry Kramer's head, just as it had put thousands of readers inside his head, and I had learned to share and sometimes anticipate his thoughts.

At the time of the publication of *Instant Replay*, I wrote a letter that was sent to dozens of sportswriters along with a copy of the book. The letter went out over Jerry Kramer's signature, even though, unlike every word of *Instant Replay* and *Farewell to Football*, the phrases did not spring straight from his recordings. My wife read the letter. "It's scary," she said. "You write the way he talks."

Now if I can only learn to block.

DICK SCHAAP

New York City, May 1969

Introduction

Of all the reactions to the publication of my first book, *Instant Replay*, the one that seemed to me the most sincere came from Alex Karras, my good friend on the Detroit Lions. In *Instant Replay*, I had humorously called Alex a nearsighted hippopotamus. When we renewed our friendship on the football field last fall, Alex naturally wanted to return the compliment. As I missed a 52-yard field goal attempt against the Lions, Alex burst through our blockers, brushed past me and, in horrible, muffled, bull-like tones, grunted, "Stick *that* in your book, you———."

What really hurt me was not Alex's rather harsh opinion, but the discovery, several months later, that he had not even read *Instant Replay*. After the 1968 season ended, I bumped into Wayne Walker, once my classmate at the University of Idaho and, for the past ten years, Alex's teammate on the Lions. Wayne told me that before the Lions played Green Bay, he had walked up to Alex and said, "Alex, did you see what Jerry said about you in his book?"

"No," Alex confessed.

"He said that you quit," said Wayne, trying to steam Alex up. "He said that you give up. He said that you don't try when we get far ahead or far behind. That's what he said."

Alex thought it over for a while. "Well," he said, finally, "Jerry's right about that."

I hope that by now someone has read the book to Alex.

In *Instant Replay*, I had paired Alex with Merlin Olsen as the toughest tackles I've faced, and Merlin, more than Alex, found the book a source of inspiration. Merlin was inspired to kill me. I'd written that, on Travis Williams' 46-yard touchdown run against the Los Angeles Rams in the 1967 Western Conference championship game, I'd blocked Merlin to the inside. What I'd said was true, but I guess it wasn't the whole truth. Travis broke through a hole pretty far away from Merlin and me, and I suppose it wouldn't have made any difference what I did with Merlin. Some newspaperman told Merlin what I'd written, and Merlin got upset. He resented the implication that I'd taken him out of the play. "Wait till we play the Packers," Merlin told the newspaperman. "I'll show Kramer an instant replay."

When we played the Rams in Milwaukee, Merlin and I had quite a battle. He must have gotten the better of it, because the Rams beat us 16–14. After the game, I saw Merlin at the airport, and he had a copy of *Instant Replay* under his arm. He told me that he had bought the book after the newspaperman spoke to him, that he and his wife had both read it and had both enjoyed it and that he wasn't mad at me at all. He had even enjoyed my dreams about stomping him into the ground. Merlin certainly has a better sense of humor than Alex has.

Most of the reaction to the diary from within football was very favorable. On the field in San Francisco, just before we played the 49ers, John David Crow, who has been a great player for the 49ers for a decade, came up to me and asked me if I'd do him a big favor. "Sure," I said.

"Would you send me an autographed copy of the book for John David, Jr.?" said Crow. "That's the only thing he wants for Christmas."

I was really moved by that, and after I said I'd do it, the 49ers proceeded to beat us out of a chance to win the National Football League championship. I still sent John the book.

My teammates generally liked the book. Claudis James said, "Boy, it'll be a great way for me to remember my rookie season ten years later," but Lee Roy Caffey said he was going to sue me for calling him a big, fat, lazy turkey. Lee Roy was only kidding, I think. Besides, he's not fat.

I was really worried, of course, about one man's reaction to the book. He's the toughest literary critic in the country—Vincent Thomas Lombardi. I gave every man on the team a copy of the book as soon as it came out, but I didn't give one to Lombardi. I wasn't sure how he'd take to some of my frank descriptions of him.

About four or five games into the season, Marie Lombardi, Vince's wife, walked up to me and said, "Where's my book?"

"I've been meaning to give you one," I said. *If you promise not to show Vince that line about the short, fat Italian*, I thought.

"Well, I want it," Marie said, "and I want it autographed."

I spent a full week sweating over the inscription to coach Lombardi. I finally wrote: "To Vince Lombardi, against whom I and all others shall forever be measured."

I gave the book to Vince, and he took it home and let Marie read it. The next week, in a hotel in Milwaukee, when I stepped into an elevator, Vince and Marie and about ten of their friends were in there. I stood next to Marie.

"Jerry," she said, "I just loved the book. It's marvelous. I enjoyed it tremendously. It's helped me to understand."

"What?" I said. "Me—or football?"

"Him," she said. "After twenty-eight years, it's helped me to understand him."

I don't know whether Vince ever got around to reading the book himself, but later Marie told me that she had read parts of it aloud to him. She said that when she read the section after the Baltimore game, where Bart Starr was talking about how brilliantly coach Lombardi had prepared us for the game, Vince had tears in his eyes.

The book brought me a great deal of pleasure. It made me hundreds of new friends, good friends, and I started watching the best-seller lists as carefully as I watched the NFL standings, which may help to explain why I had a better year in the publishing business than I did in the football business.

Now I'm out of the football business, and with this book, to my surprise, I'm taking another shot at the publishing business. When *Instant Replay* came out, I figured that was the beginning and the end of my literary career. But then a lot of people wrote to me and talked to me and told me their only complaint was that the book ended too soon, that they wanted to read more. I was shocked. One of the reasons I'd written a book was to answer my own question, "Why do I keep playing football?" I thought I'd answered the question, at least to myself, and I didn't expect other people to want to know more.

I guess I want to know more, too. I want to get an overall look at myself. I'm making a big transition now, maybe the biggest move I'll ever make, and I want to understand exactly what I'm doing and why I'm doing it. I just want to know myself a little better.

This book has to be very different from *Instant Replay*. That was my diary of a beautiful season, a perfect season, and I never knew till the last day how it would turn out. It was immediate. It was instinctive. Now I want to be reflective, introspective.

I'm in a totally new position. No more shots of novocaine to kill my pain. No more helmet to scrape my forehead raw. No more 280-pound tackles trying to crack my ribs. I'm a civilian. I'm a businessman. Yet I know that all that I learned in football, all that I learned from Vince Lombardi, I'm going to be using the rest of my life. "Winning is not the most important thing," Vince always said. "It is the only thing."

Vince taught me to be a winner. Vince taught me the value of excellence. This book, then, if it is about any one thing, is about the pursuit of excellence. It is about what I suffered, and what I enjoyed, on the way to the top of one profession. It is also about the agonies of the loss of excellence, the despair of my final season. It is a look backward, all the way to my childhood in Montana and Utah and Idaho, but, even more important, it is a look forward.

I am, I guess, a typical product of Vince Lombardi. I don't ever want to finish second at anything.

JERRY KRAMER

Green Bay, Wisconsin
April 1969

1

A Part of Yesterday

IT WAS A cold, cloudy day late in the 1968 season, and we were playing the New Orleans Saints in Milwaukee. We had just lost two straight games, to the Chicago Bears and the Minnesota Vikings, crucial games, games we had to win to have a good chance to capture the Central Division championship of the National Football League. For more than a month, I had been wearing a cast on my right hand, a reminder of a broken thumb suffered against the Atlanta Falcons. My right knee ached, the result of some ligaments torn during our second game with the Detroit Lions. Mentally, too, I was dragging.

I just couldn't get excited about playing against the Saints. As bad as we had looked lately, they didn't figure to give us much trouble. I went out on the field before the game and went through the calisthenics, just as I had been going through the calisthenics for nineteen years of high school, college, and professional football.

I shouted at my teammates, "C'mon, c'mon, let's go, let's get 'em!" and I listened to their shouts. And I looked up at the press box.

Vince Lombardi was sitting in the press box. Paul Hornung was sitting in the press box. So were Max McGee and Jimmy Taylor and Fuzzy Thurston. For nine years, from 1959 through 1967, Vince Lombardi had been my coach on the Green Bay Packers. For nine years, Paul Hornung had been my teammate and, more than that, as strange as it sounds, my favorite football player. For most of a decade, Jimmy Taylor's locker had been the one right next to mine in the dressing room. Max McGee's locker had been on the far side of Jimmy's, and Fuzzy Thurston's had been on the far side of Max's.

Now Vince was the general manager of the Packers, no longer our coach. Paul had his own radio and television shows in Chicago. Jimmy was a scout for the New Orleans Saints, and Max and Fuzzy were in the restaurant business together in Wisconsin. I stared up at all of them, clustered together in Lombardi's isolation booth, all dressed in civilian clothes, and somehow I felt that I belonged up in the press box too. That was yesterday up there in the press box, and I was a part of yesterday. I didn't belong to today. I didn't belong on the playing field.

Right then, I guess, deep inside me, I knew that I would retire at the end of the 1968 professional football season.

I wouldn't admit it, even to myself. I'd been kidding myself all season, telling myself that we were going to win, telling myself that I still had all my speed and all my ability, telling myself that I had three or four years left to play. Hell, I was only thirty-two years old. When I got too slow to play guard, I could shift over to tackle. And I could always place kick. Hadn't I made my first four field goal attempts of the season? One of them was from 38 yards out, another from 35, pretty fair kicks. (Never mind that I'd missed the next five in a row.) I kept kidding myself right down to the end of the season. Even then, I told everybody that I felt the Packers had the ability to bounce back in 1969. I told everybody that I felt I had the ability to bounce back in 1969.

Still I didn't commit myself to playing in 1969. I promised myself and my friends that I'd make my decision by May 1. Yet I hinted, even to myself, that I was going to come back. I told myself how hard I'd work to get myself in shape. In recent years, I hadn't done anything in the off-season to get in condition, nothing more strenuous than a few rounds of golf. But 1969 was going to be different. On May 1, I was going to start working out three to five times a week. I was going to lift weights and I was going to run, and I was going to get myself in the condition I should have been in five years ago. I was going to work that fat off my legs and off my gut. I was going to play at 243 pounds, not at 255. I knew that in the past few years, I had allowed my business interests to interfere with my football, so I decided that on May 1, if I chose to play, I was going to put all my businesses in the hands of my attorney. I was going to make a total commitment to football.

While I delayed my decision, I traveled around the country. I spoke at banquets. I attended the inauguration in Washington. I enjoyed myself. I was trying to take it a little easy, but business propositions kept cutting into my relaxing time. I went to New York and talked to Roone Arledge, the director of ABC-TV sports. We talked about my working on college football telecasts; we talked about my doing other television shows, especially the American Sportsman. Roone mentioned the possibility of sending me on a Bengal tiger hunt in India; I couldn't imagine anything more fun. I also talked to Bill MacPhail, the president of CBS-TV sports, and while he told me that, because of the contractual arrangement between CBS and the NFL, he couldn't offer me anything specific until I actually retired, he indicated that someday he'd like to use me on pro football telecasts. I was flattered by the interest of both ABC and CBS, but I couldn't commit myself or ask them to commit themselves because, in the back of my mind, I was still thinking about playing football.

My other business interests also kept me busy. A major oil company made a bid to buy out the offshore diving company I had helped found in Louisiana. If the deal went through, the oil company wanted me to keep working with them. At the same time, I was getting deeper into the restaurant business, with pieces of four restaurants in Colorado and Illinois, and deeper into the real estate business in Oklahoma. The more I moved around, the more people I met, and the more people wanted to help me and advise me. At least half a dozen companies implied that I could go to work for them. I got so much attention that I figured somebody must have got me mixed up with a quarterback.

My head was swimming from all the possibilities, and slowly—slowly, because I wanted it to be slowly— I began to realize that I couldn't play football in 1969, that I simply couldn't afford to put another year into football. It was a terribly agonizing realization. Sooner or later, of course, everyone who plays pro football must quit. For the player, rare these days, who has no outside business interests, the decision is relatively simple. He keeps playing until his coaches or his doctors tell him that he is no longer able to meet the demands of the game. For the more typical player, who is thinking about coaching or selling insurance or stocks full time, the key to his decision is timing. He has to make certain that he does not get out too soon or too late, that he takes maximum advantage of opportunities on and off the field. I was in a fairly unusual position, a strong position. I had no financial worries about getting out of football. I knew that I could make a living a dozen other ways. This should have made my decision easy. It didn't.

The worst part, I think, is giving up the way of life. It is a beautiful way of life, sharing setbacks and triumphs with a group of guys whose interests, if not the same as your own, are at least similar. I've said before that what I like best about pro football is the camaraderie, and I mean it. Basically, I like all kinds of people, and I like meeting new people, but no matter what I do from now on, no matter where I go, I doubt that I'll ever be so close again to a group of people as I was to my teammates on the Green Bay Packers. We laughed together. We swore together. We struggled together. Sure, we laughed at stupid things sometimes, and we swore unnecessarily, and we struggled to play a silly game. We were big kids in many ways. But, damn, it was fun.

Nothing will ever match the feeling of that championship game against the Dallas Cowboys in 1967, from the sheer exhilaration of that final drive toward our winning touchdown to the crazy, childish evening that followed. Remember, we were playing in thirteen-degrees-below-zero weather, but on that winning march, when I knew we were going to score, the adrenalin flowed so strongly I forgot the cold. I forgot everything but the feeling of eleven men working together, trying to do everything in harmony. And I can still feel the pure pleasure of the scoring play, when Ken Bowman and I blocked Jethro Pugh, the ecstasy of seeing Bart Starr squeeze by me into the end zone, the slaps on the back and the yells and the blood pumping so hard right into the locker room. And then that night, I got silly drunk, singing songs with Fuzzy in his restaurant, with the heating system broken and the temperature down to twenty-two below, and all the wives and the dates and the nonplayers shivering, and the rest of us still warmed by the heat of victory. What a night! I wore a black suit cut so that I looked like a Mississippi riverboat gambler, Gaylord Kramer. I've never worn that suit since, and I probably never will, but I couldn't throw it away.

Giving up football is giving up that day. It is also giving up the hero's role. I worry about that. I wonder how much I'll miss being recognized, being congratulated, being idolized. For years, as an offensive lineman, I worked in relative obscurity, but with the block against Jethro Pugh and with the success of *Instant Replay*, I became as well known as a running back. I was recognized in restaurants, on the golf course, in the streets, and I loved the strange, sweet taste of recognition.

I know that the fan's memory is not long, that my name will fade quickly, that in a few years I'll sink back into anonymity. I have to wonder how I'll react to that. I've seen so many ex-football players desperately trying to recapture their glory, so eager to have you listen to them for five minutes or ten minutes or an hour so that they can tell you what they did and what it was like. It's sad, very sad. I don't think I'll be like that, but I can't tell for certain. You get spoiled, being a celebrity. I've been spoiled, particularly, because I've been kind of a half-celebrity, not bothered so much it got to be a pain, not pursued like a Sinatra or a Mantle or a Namath to the point where I had no privacy at all. I was pursued just enough to keep my ego well fed. I hope I don't need the ego-gratification to survive, but I just don't know. I won't know for a few years.

I thought about the loss of the football life and the loss of recognition, and still I knew that I should retire. For some guys, retirement may be a luxury, but for me, playing football in 1969 would have been, despite the physical demands, a luxury, a self-indulgence. I faced too many opportunities to turn my back and retreat into the isolated world of professional football.

I'm introspective. I like to examine and cross-examine my own motives, and I suspect that maybe one of the reasons that I even considered playing another year was that I didn't want to test myself outside football, that maybe I wanted to use football the way some guys use an army career, to escape decisions and responsibilities. And, if I'm going to be honest with myself, I've got to admit that the thought of the training schedule I had set for myself, the heavy workouts beginning in May, didn't exactly thrill me. The more I thought about it, and the more I looked at my fat legs, the less appealing it seemed. I couldn't imagine enjoying it.

Yet I hesitated to retire for one more reason, for a reason that has prolonged too many athletic careers. I didn't want to go out a loser. Jimmy Brown retired from football perfectly; he quit at his absolute peak, before either age or defeat tarnished his great reputation. I'd been an All-Pro member of a world championship team in 1966 and 1967, but in 1968 I'd been neither All-Pro nor a world champion. The idea of trying one more year, trying to make All-Pro for the sixth time and trying to win a sixth NFL championship, had its appeal. But then I thought of all the guys who've tried to hang on, who've tried to regain their peaks after their skills had left them. Joe Louis is probably the classic example. As great as he was, he really hurt his image by competing too long. There've been so many guys who told themselves, after a bad season, I'll just play one more year, one more good year, and then I'll get out. They were kidding themselves; they never regained their skills. I realized that the odds had to be against me ever being All-Pro again, and the odds had to be against the Packers regaining the world championship. I made up my mind, finally, definitely, absolutely, that I would quit.

I considered discussing my decision with Vince Lombardi, but he had already moved to Washington to take over his new duties there as coach and general manager of the Redskins. If I'd had a reason to go to Washington, I'm sure I would have tried to see him. I have tremendous respect for Vince's opinions. At the end of the 1967 season, he practically forced Fuzzy Thurston into retirement; he saw Fuzzy at a banquet and said bluntly, "When are you going to announce your retirement?" For a while, Fuzzy hated Vince for pushing him into retirement, but now, I'm pretty sure, Fuzzy is grateful. Thanks to Vince, Fuzzy got out at just the right time, while he was still on top.

I didn't have any good reason to travel to Washington, and I didn't think a telephone conversation would do any good, so I skipped a discussion with Vince. Instead, as soon as I had made up my mind, right after a golf tournament in Florida, I flew to Green Bay to tell Phil Bengtson, our coach. I flew more than a thousand miles without phoning Phil in advance, and when I got to Green Bay, I found out he was in Scottsdale, Arizona. I guess that's typical of the intelligence of an offensive lineman.

When I couldn't reach Phil by phone in Arizona, I decided to wander over to Lambeau Stadium, just to look around at the place where I'd played so many football games. I took my two sons, Tony and Danny, with me, went to the locker room, and walked over to my locker, with my name and my uniform number above it in gold lettering against a green background. I looked at my name plate, and at the one next to mine—Travis Williams, ten years younger than me— and once more I felt that I was a part of the past. I wanted to take the name plate down and bring it home as a souvenir, but somehow I couldn't. I told myself I'd take it the next time I came to the locker room. I looked at that empty stall and, for a moment, I wondered how I'll feel the first time I see somebody else in a Green Bay uniform wearing 64, the number I'd worn for fifteen years of college and pro football. He'll be big and strong and young, and I'll hate him for his youth and his strength.

Doug Hart was in the locker room. Doug's a defensive halfback—we call him L'il Brother because he never weighs more than 182 or 183 pounds—and he's been one of my closest friends on the team. Doug was picking up some equipment for a basketball game. A bunch of the Packers play basketball exhibitions in the winter; I used to play a little myself.

Doug told me that all the guys were meeting at the shopping center, so I drove over there and saw Zeke Bratkowski and Boyd Dowler and Jim Flannigan and Jim Weatherwax and Forrest Gregg. Forrest had announced a few weeks earlier that he was retiring to become an offensive line coach for the Pack. For most of my years at right guard, he'd played next to me at right tackle.

I said hello to everybody and asked Forrest a little about his coaching duties. He told me he'd be getting himself in shape, too, and if he had to play, he would. Then he said, "Well, Jerry, I got to ask you." Forrest didn't have to spell out the question.

"I don't think I will," I said.

"Are you sure?"

"Yeah," I said, "I'm pretty definite. I'm trying to reach Phil to tell him."

"I'm sorry to hear it, Jerry," Forrest said, "but I realize you got a lot of things going."

We visited a little while, and already I felt like an outsider. I drove back to the farm I've bought near Green Bay, and I spent most of the night thinking about what it was going to be like not playing football any more, not being with the guys, not hearing the crowd yelling. I felt more than a little sad.

The next day, Henry Jordan, who's lived right across the street from me in Green Bay for several years, came out to the farm to see me, and I told Henry I was going to retire. "I'm probably going into television work or the diving company or both," I said.

"If I had something else to do," Henry said, "I'd sure retire, too."

Henry sat there at my farm talking to me, and he looked tired and he looked heavy and, by football standards, he looked old. He's thirty-four now, and he's going into his thirteenth professional season, and I really felt sorry for him. Henry's had a bad back for a few seasons now, a back that just kills him sometimes, that makes football torture. For at least five years, from 1960 through 1964, he was the best defensive tackle in pro football, but now he's slowed down, and he doesn't know for sure what he wants to do after football, and this fall he's going to go out on the field and the fans are going to say, "Poor old Henry, poor old Jordan." And all the time, while I was talking to Henry and feeling bad for him, I couldn't help being very happy that I had prepared myself, that I had something else to go to from football.

The next day, in Green Bay, I bumped into Tom Miller, our assistant general manager. "How's everything?" he said.

"I think I'm going to head south," I said.

"Full time?"

"Yeah. I think I'm going to retire."

"Well," said Tom, "we're sure going to miss you."

It was strange; nobody seemed very upset about my decision to retire. Nobody tried to talk me out of it. I was a little hurt. I guess I expected a little more emotion, a little more argument from people. Instead, they just said, "Well, we're sure going to miss you" as casually as they'd say "Hello" or "See you later."

I flew back to Florida for a speaking engagement, and, from Florida, I finally reached coach Bengtson on the phone in Arizona. I don't suppose he thought I'd called to chat about the weather, but we did, anyway, and we compared golf scores. He told me he'd been shooting over 100, and I lied and told him I had, too. I don't know whether I was trying to make him feel better, or whether I was just trying to build up a bet for the future. Come to think of it, maybe Phil was building up his handicap, too.

"I think I'm going to retire, Phil," I said. "At least I'm going to try to retire." It was funny the way I couldn't come flat out and say I was never going to play again.

"I'm sorry to hear it," Phil said, "but I'd kind of expected it. I know your time's being demanded by a lot of other interests."

Phil was friendly and helpful and understanding, just as he's always been, and he suggested that I time the announcement of my retirement very carefully, to get the maximum benefit for my other interests. Phil didn't try to talk me out of quitting either. It kind of reminded me of something Cotton Barlow, my high school coach in Idaho, used to say. "If you think you're going to be missed," he'd say, "go over and put your foot in a bucket of water. The hole that you leave when you take your foot out is about as much as you'll be missed."

It's over now, it's done, and I'm afraid I won't be missed. Maybe a little, by Alex Karras or by Merlin Olsen, and maybe a little by the fans, but not for long. I'm going to miss football a lot more than it's going to miss me. The one consolation is that I've got a lot of good memories to take with me.

I remember, first of all, the guys, every single one of them, from Joe Francis, the Hawaiian quarterback who was a rookie with me, to Leon Crenshaw, the big Tuskegee tackle who finally made the club last year on his third try. And next I remember the pride and the determination that became the trademark of the Green Bay Packers. The two come together, the guys and their spirit, in a single incident that always seemed to me a symbol of why we won.

We were playing the Baltimore Colts several years ago, and Fuzzy Thurston was playing opposite Big Daddy Lipscomb of the Colts. Fuzzy had come to us from Baltimore, so he knew Lipscomb pretty well. Big Daddy was a giant, about six foot eight, and on that particular day he weighed 326 pounds. During the game, Big Daddy kept saying to Fuzzy, "Listen, man, you're holdin' Big Daddy, cut that out." Offensive linemen are sensitive about being accused of holding, and I know that Fuzzy very rarely did it intentionally, maybe once every couple of years or something like that. He hated being accused. But Big Daddy kept telling Fuzzy he was holding him, and then Big Daddy started telling everyone else. He turned to Jim Ringo, our center and captain, and he said, "Ringo, you tell that Thurston to quit holdin.' That man's been holdin' Big Daddy the whole game. Tell him to cut it out." And then Big Daddy looked at the referee and said, "Referee, that Thurston's still holdin' Big Daddy. Been holdin' all day." Fuzzy got madder and madder, and, finally, he pulled himself up to his full five foot eleven and maybe 255 pounds—giving away nine inches and 70 pounds—and turned to Lipscomb and said, "Big Daddy, shut your ass." Fuzzy had his fist clenched. He was ready to fight Big Daddy. It was a comical picture, the stump and the giant, but it was a mark of Fuzzy's fierce pride.

There are so many beautiful memories. Emlen Tunnell, who was always bragging about the great black athletes, about Willie Mays in baseball and Wilt Chamberlain in basketball and Sugar Ray Robinson in boxing, explaining to me one day why there were no great black skiers or hockey players: "Did you ever see a black snowman?" Max McGee, whose wit was as quick as his hands, after listening to Vince Lombardi tell us that we were going to play in Cleveland Stadium before more people than live in all of Green Bay and that we might get scared, shouting out: "Hell, coach, the only thing that scares me is that the Browns might not show up." Jimmy Taylor, when asked, after his brutal head-to-head battle with Sam Huff of the Giants in the 1962 championship game, whether Huff had said anything to him during the game, getting off probably the one funny line of his career: "Huff didn't say nothing, but he should have kissed me, he was on top of me so much." Fuzzy Thurston, after watching Donny Anderson, the $600,000 bonus boy, run over and knock out Kansas City's Fred "The Hammer" Williamson in the first Super Bowl game, cheering: "You must've hit him with your purse." Willie Davis, after coming out of a fairly confusing conversation with coach Lombardi, shaking his head and saying: "Vince is my man, he's my man. Only my man don't tell the truth all the time." Paul Hornung, always Lombardi's favorite pupil, his prize product, explaining how much he respected Vince's judgment: "If he told me to run around end, climb into the stands and start selling programs, I'd do it. We might even score a touchdown that way."

I really have no major complaints about my football career, but I'd like to be able to wipe out one memory, the memory of the 1968 season. It was our first losing season in ten years, our first losing season since my rookie year. It hurt. Once you have reached the peak of excellence, nothing hurts more than the loss of excellence. It was hardly the most eloquent way for me, a celebrated author, to say good-by to football.

2

The End of an Era

I WATCHED Gene Hickerson come out on the field, watched him test his cleats against the turf, watched him move his legs up and down, watched him rub his hands together, and all the time, from a vantage point atop the roof of Cleveland Stadium, I knew exactly what he was feeling, exactly what he was thinking. I had a horrible empty feeling. I felt lonely. I felt lost. For the first time in eleven years, I was attending a professional football game in which the Green Bay Packers were not playing.

The Cleveland Browns, with Gene Hickerson at right guard, were meeting the Baltimore Colts for the championship of the National Football League, and I was in an open shed on the roof of the stadium, getting whipped by the wind off Lake Erie, working as a television commentator for station WLUK-TV, Green Bay.

I had awakened early that morning of December

29, 1968, my stomach churning as nervously as if I had been playing in the game myself. The tension carried right through the entire game. Only during time-outs and at half time did I really feel the cold of the day.

The game began, and I watched Gene Hickerson, All-Pro right guard, working against Billy Ray Smith of the Colts, experiencing as much trouble with Smith as I often had. I watched Dan Sullivan, the right guard of the Colts, working against Walter Johnson, the bruising defensive tackle of the Browns who had always impressed me with his strength, handling Johnson well, helping to open big holes for Tom Matte to crash through. I studied the line play, studied what I knew best, and whenever someone got in a particularly good lick, I could feel the vibrations way up on the roof. In my mind, I pulled, I trapped, I pass-blocked, and I suffered. I suffered an enormous sense of loss.

I watched Johnny Unitas on the sidelines, manning the phone to the coaches in the press box, forced out of action, his arm no longer half of what it once was. Johnny's always been kind of an idol of mine, the type of ballplayer I admire tremendously. He's a little like Arnold Palmer; the way Palmer used to charge a golf course, Unitas charged a football game. He always went for victory. It's just about all over for him now, and I identified with him. I shared his helplessness.

It was so frustrating, perched on the roof, a spectator after winning three straight NFL championships and five in seven seasons. Not until that afternoon did I fully realize how much I, and all my Green Bay teammates, had surrendered during the 1968 football season. I wished right then that every member of our team could have sat up there with me, and felt what I felt, and if, by some miracle, we all could have watched the 1968 title game before the 1968 season began, I'm positive the season would have been different.

For the Green Bay Packers, the 1968 NFL season was a disaster.

From 1965 through 1967, we lost a total of only nine games; we won, including playoff contests, thirty-eight games. In 1968, we lost seven games, and we won only six. Everybody, it seemed, had his own explanation for what went wrong. Some people said flatly that the sole difference was the absence of Vince Lombardi, who, after nine years as coach and general manager, had decided to devote himself completely to the general manager's job. Some people insisted that the Packers had simply gotten too old to do the job.

I don't think a simple explanation works. I think the answer is far more complicated. I've always felt that football is a game of inches, and in 1968, the Green Bay Packers lost a lot of inches: Our place-kicking was far off its 1967 form—minus one inch there; we were hit heavily by injuries, particularly in the defensive line—minus a second inch; we missed Lombardi's inspirational genius—minus a third inch; we missed Lombardi's tactical offensive brain—minus a fourth inch; we didn't seem to get our share of the breaks in officials' calls and the bounce of the ball—minus a fifth inch. We lost too many inches.

But a plain straight rule really isn't enough to explain our decline. You've got to use a slide rule. There were fractions of inches lost within the inches.

At the start of the season, I never suspected we were heading for such a fall. I knew I was getting older, and I knew that many of our players were getting older, but I still felt certain that we were strong enough to dominate the Central Division. It didn't look like a tough division. Detroit, Chicago, and Minnesota all had major weaknesses; not one of them had a particularly gifted quarterback.

The retirement of coach Lombardi, and the elevation of Phil Bengtson, our defensive coach for nine years under Lombardi, to the head coaching job didn't seem an insurmountable blow. Nobody thought Phil would be another Lombardi—he's a totally different sort of man, a gentler man, a calmer man—but we all knew that Phil was dedicated to perfection every bit as much as Lombardi was. Our defensive team has always been a reflection of Phil's brilliance, a magnificently co-ordinated, magnificently trained unit. And the defensive players loved Phil; to a man, they wanted to win for him. I know I felt a great deal of affection for Phil, even though I had never played directly under him, and once, early in the season, I mentioned to Jim Weatherwax, a defensive tackle, "We've got to win this game. We've got to have a good season for Phil."

"Yeah, we want to win for Phil," Wax said. "And we also want to win to show everybody that it wasn't just Lombardi these past few years, that it wasn't all him, that we can have a good season without him."

I suppose several of the guys had that feeling, a resentment that Lombardi had gotten too much credit for their efforts. I never felt that way myself; I honestly felt that Vince was the difference between a good team and a great team. In professional football, the teams are just about equal physically; all of them have players with strength and size and speed. The big difference between winning and losing, I think, is motivation, and nobody'll ever deny that Vince motivated us. He made us hate him much of the time, but even this hatred, this half-serious suspicion that he treated us all like dogs, served to unify us. We had a single target for all our frustrations, and maybe that's one of the fractions we lost in 1968.

Our training camp got started a little late because of the players' strike. While we were on strike, Jim Weatherwax and Bart Starr led us in workouts at a local high school field for a few days. Looking back,

I'm afraid that they worked us harder than the coaches did.

I know that Dave Hanner, the defensive line coach, suggested to coach Bengtson that he make the first three days of training camp the most punishing we had ever gone through, that he whip us and whip us and whip us so that we'd know it wasn't going to be easy just because Vince was gone. But, apparently, Phil decided that he wasn't Lombardi and he wasn't going to follow Lombardi's path. Our training camp looked like a Lombardi camp, the same schedule, the same drills, the same plays, but it was just a little looser, a little more lax. We kept telling each other that we were working just as hard as we did under Lombardi, but I don't think any of us really believed it. The obvious difference was the grass drills, the murderous up-down exercises. Under Lombardi, they were the most excruciating torture, and we did sixty or seventy of them at a time, till we were all ready to die. But in training camp in 1968, we did maybe fifteen or sixteen up-downs at a time.

Some of the guys definitely took advantage of Phil. He gave us water breaks and Gatorade breaks, things we'd never had before, and guys would sneak over in the shade sometimes and lie on the ground. Nobody ever took a breather when Vince was around. And the first week of training camp, a rookie snuck out of camp. Can you imagine a rookie sneaking out of a Lombardi camp? Vince would have yelled from Green Bay to Washington. The kid got caught, and he got hit with a heavy fine, a $1,000 fine. He was cut before he ever paid off the full fine, but his $10 per diem was withheld as long as he stayed in camp, and I heard rumors the club wasn't even going to pay his fare home.

All through training camp and the exhibition season, we had more infractions of rules than we usually had. Bob Hyland, the second-year center, missed a bus before a game once, and he and a bunch of other guys missed a curfew another time, and one of the rookies lost his black playbook. I can't remember anybody ever losing a playbook before. There was just a slight shoddiness among the guys, a barely perceptible carelessness.

We lost two of six exhibition games, but that didn't bother us very much. We'd lost a couple of exhibitions in 1966, and that may have been the best season we ever had, fourteen victories and two defeats, one by one point and the other by three. We opened the 1968 season against the Philadelphia Eagles, and we beat them 30–13 in a sloppy game. I had a momentary feeling that things weren't as sharp and as precise as they should have been, that the team had lost a fraction of a beat; we weren't loafing, but we were missing some tiny emotional factor. Still, I wasn't too upset. We'd always been sloppy against weak teams, and we didn't realize then how bad the Eagles actually were. We should have run them off the field. Three times, we had scoring drives stopped, and we had to settle for field goals; that should have been a clue.

I was pretty happy with my own showing in the game. Donny Chandler had retired before the season, and I had taken over the place-kicking. Against Philadelphia, I kicked three extra points and three out of three field goal attempts. After the first week of the season, I was one of the leading scorers in the National Football League.

I felt like I was going to have a hell of a year financially. In 1967, I had earned $27,500 for my regular season pay. In 1968, I negotiated a pretty unusual deal. I started with a salary of $26,000, but I also got a $2,500 bonus for signing and $3,500 for scouting, and that made my actual base pay $32,500. In addition, I was to get $500 extra for each field goal I kicked (I hadn't signed my contract until after Donny Chandler, my roommate in 1967, had announced his retirement), plus a $2,000 bonus if we won eight games, another $2,000 if we won ten games, and another $2,000 if we won our division. I thought I was a cinch to earn at least $43,000. I figured I had to kick at least fourteen field goals, an average of one a game, and I figured there was no way we could lose our division, no way we could win fewer than eight games. That meant $11,000 in bonuses plus my $32,000 base. And if everything went well, I thought I had a reasonable chance of kicking eighteen field goals and the team had a reasonable chance of winning ten games. Including a potential $25,000 from the playoff and Super Bowl games, I calculated that my purely football income for the 1968 season could climb as high as $74,000, way up in the quarterback brackets. I'm glad now my life didn't depend on all those dollars.

Then we played Minnesota, and the Vikings beat us 26–13. I didn't even attempt a field goal, but I missed an extra point. It wasn't blocked; I just plain missed it. The next week, Detroit beat us 23–17. I kicked one field goal that gave us a 10–0 lead in the first quarter, then missed two in a row. I started to worry a little, about myself and about our team.

I wasn't really scared. I still figured we'd finish first in our division. What worried me was a lack of emotion. We were all operating on a very even keel, not getting depressed and not getting elated, just staying at one tempo. Phil Bengtson is not an excitable man, and he didn't get us excited. He's not a frightening man, and we weren't in fear of him. Lombardi was sticking to his word; he was staying away from the practice field, letting Phil run the team. Yet I remember after the Minnesota game, Vince came into the locker room, roamed around, and grumbled, "Too damn many blue shirts in here. Too many sideburns."

I suppose Vince's comment sounds irrelevant, but I know what he meant. Take me, for instance. I was wearing a royal blue shirt, and I had a set of sideburns.

I wore the blue shirt and the sideburns because, between my weekly television show and my weekly book-signing sessions, I cared a lot about my clothes and my physical appearance. Vince made his remark because he sensed that too many of us were caring about things other than just plain winning football games. He was right, of course. We all had something going on the side; it seemed like half of us had radio or television shows. I had my TV show, Willie Davis had his, Lionel Aldridge had his, Henry Jordan had his, and Bart Starr had a radio show. We all had a million interests outside football.

Vince had spotted Willie Davis in sideburns before training camp opened, and he had persuaded Willie to shave them off. He never did get me to shave mine. Whenever Lombardi'd bring up the subject with me directly, I'd slip off the hook by kidding him. "You oughta grow some yourself, coach," I'd tell him. "You'd look great in sideburns. You'd look like a movie star." Vince'd grumble and move away, and I stuck to my sideburns.

The week after the Viking game, despite Vince's locker room comment, I still wore my royal blue shirt. When we lost that one, too, I didn't take any more chances. I wore plain white the rest of the year. I wasn't risking Vince coming in and screaming that the trouble with the Packers was Jerry Kramer's shirts.

Before our fourth game, in Atlanta, I ate dinner with Willie Davis, our defensive captain and end, and Ray Nitschke, our middle linebacker. We'd been through all the championships together, and we got to talking about the lack of emotion on the team. "Look," I said, "we've got to motivate ourselves. We're not going to get motivation from any other source. We've got to be strong enough to do it ourselves."

Willie nodded, and Ray nodded, and I nodded, but we were all just whistling in the dark. Sure we meant well, but we'd forgotten how to motivate ourselves. We'd gotten lazy under Lombardi; he'd pushed us so hard we never had to push ourselves. Willie tried; Ray tried. Willie always had been a holler guy, but Ray became one. He kept slapping guys on the back, shouting encouragement, prodding them, pushing them, but somehow it didn't work. It wasn't convincing. Some spark was lacking.

We won the Atlanta game 38–7. The score made it look easy, but with ten seconds to play in the first half, the score was still 7–7. I missed three field goal attempts in the first half, one of them from the 20-yard line. Instead of stepping in a straight line, I was stepping left to right a little bit. I kicked every ball far enough, but every ball sailed about two feet outside the right goal post. I lost the field goal-kicking job that day.

I broke my right thumb in the first half of the Atlanta game and had to wear a cast on it the rest of the year. Still, I played a full game the following week against Los Angeles; I was only one of many walking wounded. I don't know how Henry Jordan managed to keep playing week after week. He was in agony from the start of the season to the end. His back was so bad it was pathetic, absolutely pathetic, to watch him hit the blocking sled. He didn't hit it hard enough to break an egg; he couldn't. Henry went to the chiropractor every day, and he wore army boots to practice, during practice, and after practice, anything to try to straighten his back. Henry was at one tackle, and Ron Kostelnik, at the other tackle, was playing with torn ligaments. Jim Weatherwax, our only experienced reserve tackle, was out the whole season with a bad knee, and Bob Brown, who could have moved over from defensive end, broke first an arm and then a leg, so Henry and Kos had to stay in there no matter what. Jim Grabowski, our fullback, had fluid on his knee and had to have it drained almost every week—he'd go in a private room off the locker room so nobody would hear him holler—and still he never got one full game of rest. Bart Starr got off to a fantastic start; in the first four games, he completed almost 65 per cent of his passes, and then he got racked up against Atlanta. Zeke Bratkowski took over for the next couple of games, and although Zeke did his usual excellent backup job, it wasn't the same as having Bart.

The Rams beat us by two points on a field goal with less than a minute to go—we played a hell of a game against them—and the following week the Lions tied us. Six games into the season, we had a record of 2-3-1, and we were coming up against the Dallas Cowboys, by then the only undefeated team left in professional football.

We had to win the Dallas game. We played in Dallas on Monday night, and going into the game, we knew that if we won we'd be tied with Detroit for first place in the Central Division, and that if we lost we'd be in last place. Chicago and Minnesota both had records of 3-4. We met the challenge. We played the kind of football we were capable of playing. I didn't contribute much. I'd had my knee torn up in Detroit; I stretched some ligaments so badly it looked like I was going to need an operation that same night and that I was going to retire from football right then. But Jim Nellen, our orthopedic man, examined me back in Green Bay and decided to wait a couple of days, and the knee started to heal. At least I could limp, even though I couldn't think about place-kicking. I didn't practice all week, and I didn't expect to play, but when one of our guys got shaken up in the third quarter, I didn't wait to be asked how I felt. I ran out on the field. I stayed out there for two plays— didn't do anything but survive—till the coaches pulled me off. Bart returned to action, played a beautiful game, threw four touchdown passes, and we won 28-17.

Despite my injuries, I felt wonderful. We had shown

the mark of champions. We had won the game we had
to win. Now we were rolling. There wasn't any doubt
in my mind or in the minds of my teammates. We were
going to eat up the opposition the rest of the season.
Our next two games were against Minnesota and
Chicago, and we knew that if we won these two, we'd
knock both of them out of contention. Since Detroit
figured to (and did) lose its two games against Baltimore and Los Angeles those two weeks, we'd run
away from our rivals. We'd practically have the division championship wrapped up.

Our calculations were perfect—if we'd won those
two games, we'd have been champions of the Central
Division—but our playing wasn't. We lost both games.
First the Bears beat us by three points on a forty-
yard free-kick field goal with thirty-six seconds to play.
Then the Vikings beat us by four points when we
handed them three fumbles. Suddenly, instead of being
far in front of our division, we were in last place, and,
even though I'd been able to play both games, I was
very disappointed, very depressed.

Until those two defeats, we hadn't looked too much
different from some of our championship teams. We'd
played some sloppy games, but when we were winning under Lombardi, we'd almost always played a
few sloppy games. We'd been beaten by Detroit and
Minnesota, but they'd always given us rough games.
We'd looked good against the strong teams, against
Los Angeles and Dallas, and we'd won the one game
we absolutely had to win. That was always the key
to the championship Packers; we won when we had
to win. But, damn, we had to win those two games
against Chicago and Minnesota, and we didn't; it
seemed to me an indication of some deep, basic change.

I don't know if we would have won if Lombardi
had still been coaching. I tend to think that Vince,
too, would have had a hard time making us into champions in 1968. But I really missed him for those Chicago

and Minnesota games. He was the genius of the locker-room speech; he always knew exactly how to treat us. In 1967, for instance, before the Bears game that clinched the division title, he didn't say anything but a silly little joke to break the tension; a few weeks later, before the game for the Western Conference title, he quoted passionately from one of St. Paul's Epistles and really fired us up. He played us like a virtuoso.

Phil Bengtson, on the other hand, was very calm, very matter-of-fact. Before a game in 1968, we'd have our usual meeting of the players alone, without the coaches, and maybe Bob Skoronski, the offensive captain, or Willie Davis, the defensive captain, would make an emotional little speech and get us excited. Then Phil'd come into the meeting and he'd say something like, "Well, we've got to score more points." A simple, straightforward statement. Or he'd say, "I know you can win if you go out and block and tackle the way you know how to. You're a better team than you've shown so far, and if you block and tackle, you'll win." Phil never got mad at the team, as a whole, or at an individual. It just wasn't his nature. Phil's a gentleman, in the best sense of the word. Early in the year, I heard, Lombardi suggested to Phil that somebody had to be a sonuvabitch, and that if Phil wasn't going to be, one of his assistant coaches should be. But nobody picked up the responsibility to be mean. In the past, Lombardi had had enough meanness for everybody.

Phil, of course, was kept busy getting his defense ready for each game—despite all the injuries to the defense, we still had one of the best in the league—but he had to turn the offense over to his assistants. Vince had always done the same thing—giving Phil full responsibility for the defense—but Phil didn't have assistants as experienced and gifted as he had been. Ray Wietecha and Bob Schnelker tried hard, damn hard, but they were both young fellows and they couldn't possibly have the knowledge that Lombardi had accumulated over a quarter of a century. Under Lombardi, they were technicians, not strategists. All of a sudden, they were experimenting in football strategy at the same time they were experimenting in emotional motivation.

It wasn't only the coaches who were searching. The players were too. There was a new atmosphere, a strange atmosphere. I used to think a lot and talk a lot about what I called the love on our team, the feeling that each Packer had for all his teammates, and sometimes I wonder whether this spirit produced victory, or whether victory produced this spirit. I couldn't tell for sure in the past, but the events of 1968 seemed to reinforce the second theory. We had more friction among the guys than I'd ever noticed before. And this comes back, at least partly, to what I mentioned about losing Lombardi as the target for all our frustrations. We used to have one man we could take out all our animosity on, all our hatred, all our bitterness. But in 1968 we were just bitching at everybody.

There'd always been a little friendly rivalry between the offense and the defense, but in 1968 the comments were more barbed. "Can't win 'em if you don't score," Lee Roy Caffey, the linebacker, would say now and then, and his grumbling words had a sharp edge. There was even friction within the defense, and I don't think that ever happened before. Willie Davis, I know, was furious with Tommy Brown, our strong-side safety. Willie'd come steaming out of a game after somebody had scored against us on a long pass, and he'd growl, "Get that man out of there. What the hell are you waitin' for? That man's hurtin' us. He's hurtin' us. Get him out of there." Willie'd never mention any name, but everybody knew who he meant, because Tommy would have just been beaten by a receiver.

Tommy did get beat a lot, but it wasn't all his fault.

He played about the same as he always had, but in the past, although he was a little weak on long coverage, he wasn't too vulnerable. He was protected by our defensive line, which had always put on a great rush, the best weapon against a long pass; Tommy didn't have to worry much about the bomb. But in 1968, with our tackles crippled—they all probably should have been in hospital beds instead of on a football field—our opponents had the time they needed to throw long on us, and Tommy got beat several times. Willie Davis' irritability stemmed from the fact that he was forced to work extra hard at defensive end to compensate for the weakened tackles. Then Willie took out his own frustrations on the most accessible target—Tommy Brown.

The change in the attitude of Doug Hart, our top defensive backfield reserve, was indicative of the mood on the team. Doug had been a regular in 1965, but when he slipped back to a second-string position in 1966 and 1967, he remained completely dedicated to the team. He had a deep desire to help out any way he could. He filled in on the special units, like the kicking teams, and he threw himself into every situation with total commitment. But in 1968, even though he played quite a bit, he wasn't happy. He actually went to the coaches and asked them to play him or trade him. He never would have made a demand like that the year before, not when we were winning.

There was even some resentment against Bart Starr among the offensive linemen. All of us had always suspected that Bart had a tendency to hold the ball too long before he threw. There were times I'd block my man and block my man and finally release him, feeling I'd given Bart enough time to pass, and then I'd turn around and Bart'd still have the ball. My man'd get to him and I'd look bad and I'd get angry with Bart, naturally, instead of with myself. But we all knew why Bart held the ball—he hated to throw when there

was even the slightest chance of an interception—and
as long as we were winning, we realized that his rea-
soning was sound. Hell, we knew that Bart was our
bread and butter. I remember I used to kid around
once in a while and refer to Bart as "the Statue of
Liberty," because he stood still so long, but it was just
good-natured kidding, nothing vicious about it at all.
But then, in 1968, the kidding by some of the guys
lost its good nature. Nobody said anything to Bart
directly, of course, but there was more than the usual
groaning about his habit of holding the ball. It was
ridiculous—Bart had led us to too many championships for anyone to take the groans seriously—but the
bloom was off the Packer love in 1968, and a lot of
stupid things get said when an affair is ending.

We all recognized that our spirit was sagging, and
around the time of the Chicago and Minnesota games,
Bart tried to bring us all together at a team party-
meeting. Bart offered to have it at his home, but we
decided that'd be too much work for his wife, so we
scheduled the party at the Century Bowling Alley in
West De Pere, a few miles outside Green Bay. The
Century had special significance because it was our
oasis during training camp, the place we always went
for an hour or two of sanity and ale.

The purpose of the gathering at the Century was to
recapture our feelings for each other, our sense of
togetherness, but I guess you can't recapture a feeling
like that. You've just got to have it. The party was
also supposed to remind us of the hours and hours of
training camp, of all the murderous work we'd always
put in getting ready for the season, of how much we'd
lose if we didn't straighten out and win our division
championship. With such a forced, contrived atmosphere of camaraderie, the party naturally got off to
a slow start. Some guys were trying to talk up our
chances, pep each other up, and a couple of guys were
shooting pool. Francis Peay, the big offensive tackle

we'd gotten from the New York Giants before the season, was sitting by the pool table, sipping a Coke. Francis is a very sensitive guy, very intelligent, very serious, doesn't drink, doesn't chase women, very dedicated. I respect him a great deal. While he was watching the pool game, Marvin Fleming, our veteran tight end who's a little flaky sometimes, began fooling around, teasing Francis some way or another. Francis had no love for Marvin anyway, and finally, he just blew up, took his Coke and threw it in Marvin's face. "Get away from me," Francis said. "Stay away from me. Don't bug me. Get away from me."

The whole party went poof. Francis apologized to Marvin for losing his temper, then came over to me and said, "I shouldn't have done that. I know I shouldn't have. That man just bugs me." Peay felt miserable, casting extra gloom over the party, and so did just about everyone else. The party broke up a little later. It hadn't worked at all.

I didn't have any feuds with anybody during the 1968 season, but the only guy I really spent much time with was my new roommate, Willie Davis. With the retirement of Donny Chandler, who roomed with me in 1967, Willie and I sort of drifted together naturally. We were both about the same age and we liked to talk about business opportunities, so we just decided to room together. It was the first time in the history of the Green Bay Packers, far as we know, that a black player and a white player had roomed together, but we didn't think much about it. It would have been silly for me to room with some young kid. Willie and I were both getting kind of granddaddish. We were past the stage of roaming around, looking at the sights. We needed our sleep. We'd eat dinner together the night before a road game and watch television together and then, in the morning, go to the devotional service together.

Between Willie and me, our phone was ringing all

the time, and we had a regular routine. Whenever I answered the phone, I'd say, "This is Mr. Davis's suite. This is his personal secretary answering. May I help you?" He'd do the same for me when he answered, and he'd always have some of his friends coming around and he'd introduce me by saying, "This is my man, my personal secretary. Mr. Kramer, get us a drink and get us a few chairs." We got along perfectly.

Outside of Willie, I wasn't as close to the guys as I had been in previous years. Some of the guys rode me a little about *Instant Replay.* "Shame the team isn't doing as well as the book," Carroll Dale said to me one day. Carroll was kidding, but . . .

And once I overheard a couple of the players' wives talking, and one of them, whose husband wasn't enjoying his finest season, said, "Well, I don't see how Jerry Kramer can go out autographing every afternoon and still play football." The other wife responded, "It doesn't seem to be hurting *his* play at all."

I'm afraid the first wife may have been closer to the truth than the second one. I used to spend all my time on the road trips playing poker with the guys, but in 1968, I was spending my time at book stores autographing copies of *Instant Replay.* When I wasn't autographing, I was on radio and TV shows, hustling my book as hard as Truman Capote ever hustled his.

Whether my outside interests affected my play or not, I know I didn't have a particularly good season. All year, I was having trouble with my trap-blocking; I was especially atrocious on the long trap block. Ray Wietecha, the line coach, kept telling me I wasn't executing the move properly, but I lied to myself and said, "What the hell, it's not that important. I know how to do it. When the time comes, if we need it, it'll be there."

I was watching game movies one morning with Gale Gillingham, the young left guard, and I saw myself moving kind of slow, taking small, mincing steps, and, still trying to con myself, I turned to Gilly and said, "You know, I've cut down my stride a little."

"Yeah," said Gilly, "and you've lost a little speed, too, haven't you?" Gilly wasn't trying to be malicious. He was simply stating a fact. It was shortly after I'd been hurt in the game with the Lions.

But even when I'd injured my knee against Detroit, I suppose part of the reason was that I wasn't moving as fast as I used to. On a sweep to the right, I pulled and headed out there, and Jim Grabowski, who was carrying the ball, came charging up behind me. I should have been out of his way, but when he got hit, he fell forward right on my knee. The pain was miserable. It happened just a few yards from the sidelines, and I actually crawled off the field. I thought my career was finished.

For the rest of the season, I never felt right physically. I never could get down in my stance properly because of the cast on my right hand. I had a steel splint right across the end of the thumb, and there was no way I could push off powerfully, no way I could get enough leverage. It was like wearing a boxing glove and playing football. My knee never stopped aching, yet, except for the Dallas game, I did all our kicking off. I really shouldn't have. Each time I kicked, the knee hurt something fierce. And a few weeks after the Detroit game, I pinched some nerves in my shoulder, and from then on, whenever I got hit up around the shoulder or the neck, my arm would go numb. It would burn and sting all the way down the arm, and I'd have to run off the field and get the trainer to rub my arm for a minute or two to get the feeling back. Then I'd trot out on the field again. I certainly didn't enjoy the season in any way.

I wasn't the only one starting to feel my age. We all tried to kid our way around the age problem. Forrest Gregg and I were talking one day early in the season, and I said, "Forrest, how do you ever know when you're too old to play?"

"You're the last one to find out," Forrest said. "Tell you what. When I'm too old, you tell me, and when I think you're too old, I'll tell you. I'll leave a note in your locker. You do the same for me." All through the season, we'd come in from practice each day and look for the note in our lockers. Forrest and I had a lot of giggles, but most of the laughter was nervous.

So many of our problems were subjective and vague —growing old, losing spirit, lacking motivation—but we had two very specific problems. One, of course, was our kicking game. After I hurt my thumb and then my knee, we went to Chuck Mercein as the kicker. Chuck was strictly a stop-gap measure. He tried two field goals and made one of them, from only twenty-one yards out. Then we turned to a kid we'd been carrying on the taxi squad, Erroll Mann. The first field goal Mann tried, against Dallas, he just barely missed. The second one, against Chicago, missed by a little more. On the third one, also against the Bears, he took a divot. That finished Mann. Mercein took over in the middle of the Bear game and again made one out of two, another short kick, from nineteen yards. The next week we started using Mike Mercer, a free agent who hadn't done any kicking for a few months. Mercer missed three of his first five attempts, then settled down and made five in a row. Still, by the end of the season, we had made only thirteen of twenty-eight field goal attempts; in 1967, Donny Chandler had made nineteen of twenty-six. Six extra field goals in exactly the right places could have changed our 1968 record from 6-7-1 to 10-4, and . . .

A second specific problem was the failure of Travis Williams, our rookie sensation of 1967, to do anything even remotely exciting in 1968. Travis averaged 41 yards a kickoff return in 1967, and 21 yards in 1968;

he scored six touchdowns in 1967, and none in 1968; he averaged 5.4 yards a carry in 1967, and 1.8 yards in 1968. His longest run of the 1968 season was 7 yards; for the full year, he gained 63 yards rushing, 25 yards less than he had gained in the 1967 Western Conference championship game alone.

As far as I'm concerned, Travis ought to be a superstar in the National Football League. He's got the speed, the strength, the ability to follow his blockers, everything. He showed up at camp before the 1967 season ten pounds underweight, still recuperating from a bad bronchitis condition, and he never really did get well. He was well enough to play, but he didn't show a thing in the games. He never even came close to breaking away once all season. When he was running well, there was never a hole. When there was a hole, he wasn't running well. He got depressed and started pressing. Instead of plugging away for four, five, six yards each carry, I think he began looking to go all the way every time, and he couldn't find an opening. His locker was next to mine. He's a good kid, a nice boy, and I felt sorry for him all year.

Not surprisingly, with all our problems, we took quite a bit of abuse from fans around the country. I got my share of it. Some guy went to a lot of trouble, clipped a bunch of my quotes out of the newspapers, pasted them up on a letter and added his own quote: "What next, loudmouth?"

Some idiot wrote an open letter to the Green Bay newspaper suggesting that if the Packers wanted to start winning again, they should bake less cookies and play more football. Without saying it, he was referring specifically to a cookie commercial that I'd done for television. What burned me was that I'd had that commercial for four years, and the first three years we'd won the NFL championship. Now we were losing because I baked cookies. I wanted to bake the guy who wrote the letter, and I wanted to boil the guys who printed it.

My weekly television show, which always included a question-and-answer segment, kept me very much aware of the mood of the local fans. I received a tremendous number of nasty letters, but the closer we came to being out of contention, the nicer most of the letters became. I had the distinct feeling that the fans wanted to motivate us with their letters, that they weren't really down on us, that they simply wanted to get us mad so that we'd play better.

After losing to Chicago and Minnesota, we did perk up a bit. We beat New Orleans and Washington, two weak clubs, without much difficulty and brought our record up to .500. The way things were going in the Central Division, we were suddenly back in the race. Chicago lost twice those two weeks to fall back to 5-6, and Minnesota split its two games to hold first place at 6-5. Detroit, at 3-6-2, was almost mathematically eliminated.

We came to the twelfth game of the season miraculously alive, facing another must game, this one against the San Francisco 49ers. By the time we took the field in San Francisco, we knew that Minnesota was going to lose to Los Angeles. We knew that if we beat the 49ers, we would be in first place in the Central Division. We had to win.

Before the game, for the first time all year, Lombardi came in the locker room and spoke to the team. He talked about how much we had to gain, how much we had to lose. He talked about the past glories of the Packers. He got emotional, of course. Vince can't say hello without getting emotional. We were up, way up, and I'm sure we'd have been up even if Vince hadn't talked to us. You didn't have to be an intellectual to realize how important this game was.

I had my confidence back. I knew we were going to win.

The first time we got the ball, we marched eighty yards for a touchdown. A little later, Bart got racked up on a blitz. Zeke Bratkowski took over for him, and in the second quarter, Mike Mercer kicked a forty-four-yard field goal to put us ahead 10–0. Five seconds before the end of the half, San Francisco cut our lead to 10–7.

In the third quarter, we moved for another touchdown, and Mercer kicked another forty-four-yard field goal, and we held a 20–7 lead entering the final period. I was absolutely positive we'd win. We had everything going. Minnesota had already lost to Los Angeles.

But the fourth quarter was a disaster, our worst collapse in all my years at Green Bay. The start of our downfall was an injury to Zeke Bratkowski. He got blitzed and battered, his back all messed up, and he had to leave the game. I'd seen Bart leave the field under his own power in the first quarter, and I was sure that now I'd see him come running back on the field. I looked at the bench, and I saw Bart, standing still, not making the slightest move to take off his warmup jacket. I suppose he'd discussed the situation with our coaches, and they'd decided he wasn't fit to play, but my heart just about broke. I wanted Bart to come running out so badly.

Instead, young Billy Stevens, a rookie from the University of Texas at El Paso, came running out on the field, and, all of a sudden, I knew we were finished. I knew we didn't have a chance. We were playing into a stiff wind, and we were tiring, and we had at quarterback a boy who hadn't appeared in a single game all year, a boy who hadn't been able to keep his poise even during practice sessions. A number of times, in workouts, without any pressure on him, he'd called the wrong play; he'd called formations we weren't even using that particular week. Hell, he was only a kid, and he was trying to play the most demanding, the most complicated position in professional football. It takes a long time to learn to play quarterback in the NFL.

Billy Stevens came to the huddle, and I said, "Oh, God," and, right away, he confirmed my worst fears. He called a play I'd never heard before. It must have been a play from back in his college days. He tried to pass a couple of times, and the 49ers hit him late and turned him on his head and stomped him into the ground and just about killed him. We couldn't move the ball at all, and each time Donny Anderson had to punt into the wind, and each time the wind pushed the ball back into our territory, and the 49ers scored 20 points in the fourth quarter and beat us 27–20.

I walked into the saddest locker room I'd ever been in. Gale Gillingham had tears trickling down his face. Phil and Vince walked around the locker room, patting guys on the head, shaking their hands, trying to lift them out of shock. We had the most terrible flight home. I felt like crying, too. An era had ended. It was all over.

Mathematically, we were still alive, barely alive; with two games to go, Minnesota and Chicago were both 6-6, and we were 5-6-1. We all had tough games coming up. We were playing Baltimore, the Bears were playing Los Angeles, and the Vikings were playing San Francisco. Baltimore had lost only one of its twelve games, but if we could beat them—we were playing them on Saturday in Green Bay—we'd still have a chance to capture our division.

We didn't quit. We worked our butts off getting ready for the Colts. In recent years, we'd always been able to beat them when we had to. In the locker room before the game, Bob Skoronski gave one of the most moving talks I'd ever heard from a teammate. His voice broke on every sentence, almost on every word

The words alone don't do justice to his feelings, but I recorded his talk:

"Fellas, I'm deeply emotional. I really can't say much. These are the things that come to my mind today. We've dedicated a lot of games over the years to coaches and people. Today, fellas, there's a lot of guys who built the Packers to what they are today who might be playing their last [home] game. I'm asking every guy here to go out and play his goddamn level best for the guys who had a lot to do with the Green Bay Packers. Boys, we're wounded, but we're not dead. If you're gonna lay down and die out there, you're going to do something I'm not going to do. I may get beat, but, goddamn, it won't be because I want to. Now let's go out there and keep our heads up and do something for the guys who've had a helluva lot to do with making the Packers, the green and gold, what they are. A lot of guys have given a helluva lot. Let's go out there and take it to somebody that's tried to take it away from us many many times. We've had a helluva lot of memories and a lot of fun, so let's go out there and take it to them. I apologize for my emotion, but that's the way I feel."

I think everybody got a little choked up by Bob's speech, and then the coaches came into the meeting, and Phil told us to go out and block and tackle and, if we blocked and tackled, we could win the game. Phil's just not an emotional man. He's a beautiful man, fair, sensitive, intelligent, a brilliant football man, but he is not an emotional man.

We ran out on the field and went through the most miserably frustrating day. We'd open up a hole, and our man'd bust through and pick up ten or twelve yards and then fumble, and they'd recover the ball. We fumbled five times and the Colts recovered four of them. It sort of summed up the whole season; every bounce went against us, every break. Donny Anderson had a punt that went three or four yards, something like that. We had only a couple of penalties against us, but they came at exactly the wrong time.

Baltimore beat us 16–3, and they had the ball with less than a minute to play, running out the clock, and I was standing on the sidelines with the rest of the offensive team, and I knew it was all over and I felt very sad, sorry for the team and sorry for myself. And then everyone in Lambeau Stadium, fifty thousand people, got up on their feet and began cheering for the Green Bay Packers, one last, long, resounding cheer, a cheer for days past. I felt chills up and down my spine. I felt grateful to the fans, and grateful for the opportunity I'd had to play for them. I felt good and bad at the same time, depressed by defeat and yet buoyed by the reaction of our Green Bay fans.

The next day, Chicago beat Los Angeles, and Minnesota beat San Francisco, and we were mathematically finished.

We had actually died the week before in San Francisco; it was only the funeral that was postponed.

Still we had to play our final game, and while it didn't mean too much to us, it was very important to our opponents, the Chicago Bears. Chicago and Minnesota were tied for first place with 7-6 records, and if the Bears could beat us, they'd win the division championship no matter how Minnesota did. The reason was that the Bears had defeated the Vikings twice during the season, and the NFL rules say that, in the case of a tie for the division title, the team that outscored the other in their two regular season games was the champion.

We played the Bear game, just as we had the Baltimore game, without Bart Starr; he really had been racked up by San Francisco. Zeke Bratkowski got hurt early against Chicago, and we brought in young Don Horn, a rookie in 1967 who had just rejoined us from the service a few days earlier. The kid played a hell of a game, led us to a 28–10 lead, and we held on to win 28–27. Minnesota won its final game, over Philadelphia, so we had the satisfaction of knocking the Bears, our traditional rivals, out of the division championship.

As long as I live, I don't think I'll forget a block I threw on Dick Butkus in that final game. I had several good blocks on him, but one in particular was perfect. I have complete respect for Butkus. He's one of the great linebackers. He's not a humpty-dumpty, and when I do something against him, I know I've accomplished something. On this one play, our center called a switch; he took the defensive tackle and I took the middle linebacker. I got off real fast, and as Butkus came drifting over, I caught him square in the chest and buckled his knees and dropped him on his backside. I flattened him. He was out of the play if the play had lasted two minutes. I never executed a better block in my life.

I was so happy with the block, and yet, in a way, I was angry, angry with myself, because that's what I should have been doing every single game. On the last day of the season, I knew for sure what I should have known all year long. I hadn't been playing up to my ability.

The day after the Bear game, just to make the season complete, my home in Green Bay burned down. My little boy, Danny, four years old, had been playing with matches, and he had started a fire in the kitchen. Fortunately, my wife, Barbara, and Danny and my two other children, Diane and Tony, weren't hurt. Fortunately, too, from an insurance standpoint, Barbara had made a complete inventory of everything in the house not long before the fire; the home of a friend of ours had burned down the year before, and Barbara, as a precaution, had decided to take the inventory. The house was almost completely ruined; it took five months to rebuild it. I was in New York, appearing on the "Tonight" show, the day the house

burned down. I wasn't even terribly surprised when
Barbara called me and told me; it was that kind of
year.

I learned many things from the 1968 season. It
wasn't a pleasant way to learn; defeat is never pleasant.
I hope, as many of us felt after the Bear game, that the
victory marked the start of a new era in Green Bay,
the start of a successful Phil Bengtson era. I know
that Phil and his assistants were working doubly hard
in the off-season to get ready for 1969. The club is
completely theirs now. Phil is general manager as well
as coach; Vince has left for Washington. Still, one of
his themes lingers, to inspire the Packers in 1969.
"The greatest achievement," Lombardi always said,
"is not in never falling, but in rising again after you
fall."

Vince's sayings meant more to me after the 1968
season. I'd accepted them before, and I'd believed
them, but I hadn't really tested them. "Fatigue makes
cowards of us all," he used to say.

We proved his point last year. Our poorest scoring
quarter was the fourth quarter; we averaged only
four points a game in the final period. It used to be
our strongest quarter. In 1967, we averaged eight
points a game, twice as many, in the fourth quarter.
If we had scored eight points in the final period of
every game in 1968, we would have won ten games.
We lost three games in the last two minutes of play.
We were tiring—becoming cowards—because we
hadn't worked hard enough to prepare for the season.
We had goofed off. We had cheated Phil. We had
cheated ourselves.

I had too many things going in 1968, too many outside interests. It didn't rob me of all my ability, but it
took away a decisive inch here, another inch there,
enough to ruin a season. I just wasn't totally committed to football, and I realize now, more than ever,
that only total commitment produces total success.

I tried to kid myself in 1968. I tried to tell myself all through the year that everything was all right, that I was playing all right, that the team was playing all right, that I was doing all I could. Nothing is more important, in football or in anything else, than to know yourself, to know your own weaknesses as well as your strengths. I ignored my weaknesses in 1968; I tried to pretend they didn't exist.

If I can remember everything I learned from the 1968 season, then the year will have been worthwhile. I won't have a chance to use those lessons in football any more, but I hope I'll be using them every day of my life.

I had a terrible experience that sort of summarized the year right after the Super Bowl game in January. I was at a gathering in Miami, and somebody introduced me as a member of the "former, former, former" world champion Green Bay Packers. Then he introduced another guy as a member of the world champion New York Jets. I burned. I hated the sound of that phrase—the former world champions. I hadn't heard it in so long. The last time the Green Bay Packers had failed to win the world championship, I had been lying in a hospital bed.

3

On the Edge of Death

IN NOVEMBER 1964, when I was a patient at the Mayo Clinic in Rochester, Minnesota, I thought seriously about killing myself. I had just had a colostomy, the most awful experience in the world. A colostomy is a horror movie that hasn't been made yet.

In very polite language, a colostomy is an incision made in the colon, which is a part of the large intestine, to create an artificial anus. I needed a colostomy in November 1964, because after a series of operations had failed to clear up a mysterious internal ailment, my large intestine had burst, my temperature had flamed up to 104, and I had felt, almost for certain, that I was going to die.

When I awakened after the emergency colostomy, my intestine was sticking out my right side, just below the ribs, a thick, red intestine, maybe two or two and a half inches in diameter, perhaps three times as big as a rubber garden hose. I don't know the exact medical procedure or terms, but the doctors had placed a glass rod underneath the intestine, pinning it so that it couldn't slip back into the stomach.

I developed postoperative pneumonia. I ran a high fever, and even though the doctors gave me injections to make me sleep, I couldn't sleep. The sheer horror of the experience, not the pain, kept me awake. A day or so after the operation, a doctor came in and, with a little burning device, which reminded me of the wood-burning kit I'd played with when I was a kid, seared a hole in the top of the intestine. The intestine was filled with stool, which smelled lovely, of course. The stool began to run out of my intestine, down my side, and into my bed. In a normal colostomy, which is performed at the lower end of the colon, the stool is reasonably well formed. But I had a high colostomy, almost an ileostomy close to the small intestine.

My nightmare had started.

They put a belt around me with a little bag attached, and when I was standing up and the stool was fairly solid, it would run into the bag. But when I was lying down and the stool was loose, it would run onto the bed. One afternoon, shortly after the colostomy, when the stool began running onto the bed, driving me insane with its odor, I rang for the nurses to change the bag and change my sheets. While they were changing the bag, the damn thing started flowing again. I had absolutely no control. I was standing up, and the stool poured out and started trickling down my leg and onto my feet and between my toes, and I couldn't stand it. I was so helpless, so humiliated.

I looked at the window. I looked very hard at the window.

I was sick, so sick, so damn sick. I was a mess, my wound draining, my intestine hanging out, my weight down from 255 pounds to under 220. I had to consider going out the window.

I didn't jump. I cried. I felt so sorry for myself. Dan Currie, one of my teammates, phoned me, and I couldn't talk to him. I choked up. I couldn't hold back the tears. I started thinking about my kids, thinking I'd never see them again. I watched "The Rifleman" on television, and I saw a scene with Chuck Connors and the little boy who always accompanied him, and I began crying again. I started making phone calls. I called my mother and my father, my brother, my closest friends from high school and college, all the people who'd meant a lot to me over the years. I didn't actually say good-by to them, but I felt I was saying good-by. I was twenty-eight years old, and I was ready to go.

My weight kept sinking. I couldn't eat. I went down to 203 pounds, the lightest I'd been since high school. I was filled with nothing but self-pity.

Then somebody mailed me a photograph that had been taken at a sports night somewhere in Wisconsin. The picture showed me and Jimmy Taylor and the guy who sent the photo. In the picture, I was wearing my world championship diamond ring and a tweed sports coat that had cost me about $165, more than I'd ever paid for a sports coat in my life, and a pair of tailored slacks, and I was smiling and happy and having a party.

And then, for some reason, my mind wandered to all the sick children I'd met during my many trips to hospitals. A few years earlier, when I'd been hospitalized in Madison, Wisconsin, for the treatment of a detached retina, I'd met a little blond-haired boy, not even three years old, and he'd had one eye removed and he had a huge lump on his forehead, a big tumor. He used to come to my room every day and tug at my fingers—my eyes were bandaged—and I'd pick him up and carry him around on my shoulders and share my basket of grapes and bananas with him. I didn't find out what was wrong with him till I was ready to leave the hospital. He died about four months later, such a sweet, cheerful little boy.

Not long before I'd gone to Mayo, I'd visited some other little children at the West Side Clinic in Green Bay. I remembered especially a little boy named Steve Jeffers, about ten years old, who had a tumor on his arm. I gave him a football as a present. Eventually, he had to have his arm amputated, and the tumor spread to his spine, and he died. I met a little boy named Mike Hoolihan, blond, four or five years old, bright for his age, who told me, "You're Jerry Kramer. I've got your football card." Mike told me he had a pain in his back, and I said, "Well, you'll be going home soon," and then a nurse told me that Mike had a tumor on his spine and he didn't have a chance. There were two little Indian children with broken legs, and I asked them what they were doing in the hospital, and they said, "We were in a car wreck. Mommy and Daddy got killed. We only had our legs broke." They were seven or eight, and they didn't realize what Mommy and Daddy being killed meant.

I thought about those children and I looked at that picture of Jimmy Taylor and myself, and I said, "You sonuvabitch, what are you feeling sorry for yourself for?"

I looked back and I told myself, "You've had a great life. You've gone more places and done more things than eighty or ninety per cent of the people in the world. You've had it pretty good. You've got no complaints." I made peace with myself.

Pretty soon after that, my fever broke. The doctors pumped me full of antibiotics, and, finally, the antibiotics killed the infection in my stomach. I found out I was going to be able to go home for Christmas. I began to suspect that I might live.

Lying in bed in the Mayo Clinic, learning to live

with my colostomy, I had a lot of time to think about my past and about my future. I thought a lot about football, naturally. I'd played the entire 1964 exhibition season and the first two games of the regular season before the doctors had discovered the tumor on my liver that started the series of operations leading to the colostomy. Now it looked as though I was never going to be able to play football again. I had lost more than fifty pounds, I was terribly weak, and, worst of all, the doctors still hadn't figured out exactly what had caused the lump on my liver.

I thought back to the last month I'd felt really healthy, June 1964. Up till then, I hadn't worried very much about my future. I'd kind of figured everything would take care of itself. I'd play football five or six more years and save a little money and invest a little money, and then I'd be able to scrape out a good enough living after football. I didn't figure I'd ever be rich, but I'd be able to go home to Idaho and hunt and fish and live a pretty nice life.

I hadn't worked very hard at securing especially good off-season jobs up till the time of my colostomy. The first few years after I'd turned pro in 1958, I'd gone home to Idaho and worked on construction-type jobs, making what I thought were good wages, but not building at all toward the future. Then, in 1964, I'd gone to work for a tire company in Madison, Wisconsin. I had some strong ideas about setting up a few big contracts and making a lot of money in commissions, and I did scout around quite a bit, but I really didn't knock myself out working. I played a little basketball and drank a few beers with the boys and played a lot of poker. The big deals didn't come through, and when I got my commission check for the month of June, the check came to a whopping $4.60. That was my full income for the month.

I was angry, angry with the company because I thought they should have paid me more for the contact work I'd done, even if I hadn't sold many tires, and angry with myself for being so damned lazy and stupid. I kept the check as a reminder. I put it under glass on my dresser.

While I was recovering from the colostomy, I thought about that check, that $4.60. I lay in bed and I came to a decision. I set myself a goal of financial independence, and I swore that I would do everything I could to reach that goal. I would put the same effort into business that I'd already put into football, so that I'd never be in a position again where I could show only four dollars and sixty cents for a full month of my life.

I promised myself that, if I had to, I'd work twenty hours a day to fulfill that commitment to financial independence, that I'd drive myself and push myself and whip myself until I achieved that goal. I know it sounds sort of melodramatic, but it was one of the crucial turning points of my life. When I left the Mayo Clinic and headed home to Green Bay, I burned with that desire for financial independence.

First, of course, I had to get myself healthy. I was still in pretty miserable shape. Henry Jordan, my teammate and neighbor, met my plane at the Green Bay airport, lifted me up as easily as if I were his little boy Butch, and carried me to his car. My legs were bony and my ears seemed oversized and my eyes were enlarged, and I looked like someone who'd just come off a death march, like one of those paintings of the hungry kids with huge eyes.

It was good to get home. I've given only the barest hint of the horrors of a colostomy. Once I got home, whenever the colostomy gave me hell, I could go downstairs in the shower and just stand there and let the damn thing go and clean up fairly easily. I still wasn't exactly independent. My wife had to change my bag for me and change my dressing and clean up my wound. Barbara had stayed with me all the time

I was at Mayo, helping to cheer me up. I'd fattened her up a little at the hospital. The doctors gave me a shot of brandy three times a day to help my appetite, and I couldn't drink the brandy—it was godawful— so I'd hide it and, at night, Barbara would drink it with a bottle of 7-Up. She looked after me like a baby. "How can you put up with all this?" I asked her once.

"Well, I've changed a baby's diaper," she said, "and this isn't really any different."

After a month of hospital food, it was great to get back to home cooking. I had a terrible craving for gravy, milk gravy, the kind my mother used to make with the cracklings off a hamburger or a steak, with a little milk and flour added to it. Barbara fed me gravy two, sometimes three meals a day, and I started feeling a little better. But I'd go downtown to a store or something, and I was all gray and bony and people would look at me as if I were dying.

And then the word spread around Green Bay that I actually was dead.

An ex-Green Bay Packer named Tom Hearden, who had played in the 1920s, had died, and when radio and television began to broadcast reports of his death, a lot of people thought they heard my name. It was an easy mistake for them to make, considering the way I looked. When the rumors started flying, I was with Bob Brault, my doctor, and he answered the phone in his office and said, "No, he's right here. Do you want to talk to him?"

I went home, and the phone rang about eight or ten times in less than half an hour, and each time my wife'd answer the phone, and the caller'd say, "How's everything?" Barbara'd say, "Fine."

"Where's Jerry?"

"Right here."

"Oh. OK. Good-by."

I got into the spirit of the thing. I called up one of

my neighbors and disguised my voice. When he said hello, I said, "Have you heard about Jerry?"

"Yes," he said. "My God, isn't that terrible?"

"Hey," I said. "This is me. This is Jerry."

"Oh," the neighbor said. "I heard he'd died."

He said "he," not "you," and I began to feel very strange, like maybe I had died and I was the only one who didn't know about it. The girl who was our regular baby sitter called, and she was in tears, sobbing, "I just heard about Jerry."

I felt I had to get out of the house, so I went down to the barber shop, and my barber did a double take when he saw me. "You were one hell of a guy fifteen minutes ago," he said. "Now you're an SOB again."

The barber started apologizing to me because he had to go to a meeting that night and he had decided that he wasn't going to be able to visit the body until the next day. "But I was getting ready to take up a collection for flowers," he said.

As long as everybody thought I was dead, I decided I might as well attend my own wake. I didn't hide like Huck Finn. I called up fifty friends and threw the wake at my own house. I bought a couple of kegs of beer, and Gary Knafelc, who'd been my teammate, brought over a headstone, and several of the guests carried ugly, wilted brown flowers. The Green Bay newspaper came out and took pictures of me and the family to prove that I was still alive.

In January 1965, I started putting a little weight back on, and I got tired of hanging around the house. Bob Brault and his wife, Suzy, and Barbara and I began going skiing. The three of them would ski, and I'd sit in the lodge, and, naturally, I got a little itchy.

The damned colostomy was an ever-present thing, much worse than a wart or a mole or even a mother-in-law. It was like a grotesque growth that clung to me. Dr. Brault and the other doctors kept telling me that I'd just have to have it another few weeks, but the time kept stretching out.

I decided I was going to go skiing. I was a pretty good skier, so I wasn't too worried about falling and hurting myself, even with the colostomy. I went over to the bunny hill, the easy slope, and after about five minutes, when I was starting to speed up, Doc Brault marched up to me and said, "What the hell do you think you're doing?"

"The hell with it," I said. "If I'm going to have this thing, I'm going to learn to live with it. I'm not going to sit on my butt." I started skiing full time, and I was falling all over the place, and I even fell on that damn thing a few times. It didn't hurt me. I just banged it up a little, herniated it a bit. The intestine stuck out more than it should have, but I just tried to ignore it. It was bad enough having to take an extra set of clothes with me everywhere I went, without letting it cramp my whole life.

All this time, while I was regaining my strength and my weight, I was moving ahead on my commitment to financial independence. I had saved up about $10,000 from football and off-season jobs, and just about the time I'd gotten really sick, in the fall of 1964, I'd made up my mind to put all the money into the stock market. Several guys told me to diversify, not to put all my eggs in one basket, but I figured, hell, I don't have that many eggs. With my $10,000, I borrowed another $20,000 and poured every cent into one stock, an over-the-counter chemical stock. The stock took off and almost doubled; by early 1965, I had $25,000 profit. I began to study investment possibilities. I bought an empty lot, planning to build a house and sell it, but that didn't work out, so I pulled out quickly. Then I put some money into buying part of an archery company in Wisconsin, the American Archery Company—I had to put up only $6,000 for the initial investment—and I looked into so many different deals my wife started calling me Corporation Charlie. I put hour after hour into examining business opportunities. I suspected strongly that I was never going to play football again, and I swore I'd excel in business. I can't stress that enough. One of the main reasons everything finally worked out was that I was totally committed. You've got to be.

Then I got a lucky break. It started out looking like just a crazy adventure, but it ended up being very profitable.

Early in 1965, I was making a little change by managing the Green Bay Packers basketball team. I couldn't play, but I booked all the games and fought over the contracts and handled the money and took my share. Urban Henry, who'd played tackle for Green Bay in 1963, was on the basketball team. Before one of our games, I started telling Urban how much success Art Laha, one of my partners in the archery company, was having with a hunting movie he'd made. Art had gone up to Alaska and had shot a lot of footage hunting polar bears and black bears and brown bears with bow and arrow. He'd edited the footage into a movie and had toured Wisconsin with it, showing it to hunting clubs and making a good bit of money.

"Why don't we make our own movie?" Urban said.

Urban had never made a movie, of course—he'd probably never touched a camera more complicated than a Brownie—but he's the sort of guy who has complete confidence in his own ability to do anything. I guess I felt pretty self-confident, too. We decided that we'd go down to the Louisiana-Texas border and make a movie hunting 'gators with bow and arrow. Urban comes from that area, from Morgan City, Louisiana. We bought a used 16 mm. Eumig movie camera and took off for alligator country. We looked around for a guide, and somebody told us that

the man in that part of the country who knew more
about alligators than anyone else was a fellow named
Sam Mutrux. We looked for Sam, but we couldn't
find him. We heard that he was down in Mexico.

Urban and I settled for a couple of young fellows
to guide us, and we brought in Jimmy Taylor, who
lived in Baton Rouge, to join us. We figured that
Jimmy would help the movie because he was a back,
and we knew that backs had box office appeal. We
were just a pair of big unknown linemen.

I still had that colostomy and my incision was still
draining, so before Urban and Jimmy and I headed
into the swamp, I stopped at a dry cleaners. I picked
up some of that plastic stuff they put around clothes,
and when I stepped into the swamp, right up to
my belly, I was wrapped up as snug as a freshly
cleaned suit.

We spent about ten days out in the swamp. We
caught a few alligators, but we didn't get very good
pictures. We had a great time. When we'd spot a
five- or six-foot alligator, he'd duck down into a hole,
and we'd chase after him in a marsh buggy, then get
out and try to find him. We'd use a pole with a hook
on it, shaped like a "J," and we'd jab the pole into
the alligator's hiding place and then try to ease him
out, nice and gentle. We managed to pry loose a few
'gators, and we managed to shoot them, but not with
a bow and arrow. We had to use a rifle. Then we took
a little artistic license. To make our movie a little
better, after we'd shot a 'gator with the rifle, we'd
shoot him with an arrow. We thought we were being
very clever, but the film wasn't much good. We really
didn't know what we were doing with the camera. As
a matter of fact, we didn't know too much about
what we were doing with the alligators either.

When we came out of the swamp, Jimmy went back
to Baton Rouge, and Urban and I met Sam Mutrux.
He told us he'd been in Mexico on business. I liked

him right away. I could tell he was the kind of man I'd enjoy working with. We tried to persuade him to go back into the swamp with us, but Sam said he couldn't. "Boys," he said, "I've got a diving contract down in Mexico and I've got to hustle up some money to get it going. I'm forming a Mexican corporation and I'm getting a contract with the Mexican government, but first I've got to speak to a bank."

Urban and I looked at each other—maybe we were a little swamp-crazy—and I said, "Look, Urban, I'd be interested in going into that." I didn't have the slightest idea what a diving contract was.

"So would I," said Urban.

We told Sam Mutrux that if he didn't come up with the money he needed from the bank, we might be able to help him out. Sam tried a few places and didn't raise any cash, so he came back to us. My stock was still going up; I figured I might as well play while the cards were running my way.

Urban and I decided to investigate the business. We jumped on a plane with Sam and flew to Mexico City, then hired a cab to drive us more than two hundred miles to Tuxpan, a town on the Gulf. We took a boat out to a drilling rig and spent three days living on the rig, trying to find out what the diving business was all about. The main job, I figured out, was to go down in the Gulf and cap wells until the oil was to be taken out of them.

Sam knew about a diving company out in the Gulf that had been working for the Mexican government, capping its wells, but was now going out of business. The company offered to sell us its equipment for about a third of its cost. I didn't have any notion of the economics involved; all I knew was that Sam Mutrux said we could make money, and he seemed like the sort of person I could trust. I've often operated by instinct, by immediate reactions to people, in my business dealings. My instincts this time were perfect.

Urban and Sam and I put up $5,000 apiece and established the Packer Diving Company. We weren't just putting the money in a gun and shooting it. With our initial investment, we did get a lot of equipment —compressors, decompression chambers, hoses, cases of tools, volume tanks—and Sam had the contract with the Mexican government.

When I went back home to Green Bay, people asked me what I'd been doing in Mexico. "I've got a diving company down there," I'd say. "Doing some diving for the Mexican government."

They'd give me a strange look, raise their eyebrows and say, "You get any money out of it?"

"No," I'd say. "Not yet."

They'd give me another look and say, "Well, I'd be careful if I were you. I'd be careful of putting my money down there."

I got so many funny looks I just stopped telling people about the diving company. I guess they figured all my operations had affected my brain.

Soon after the Louisiana trip, Bob Brault persuaded me to go back into the hospital for more exploratory surgery. My wound still wasn't healing right.

"Look, Jerry, I think we ought to operate again," Bob said. "I think there's a foreign object in there. I don't know what it is, maybe a suture, a sponge, something, something to cause the wound to keep draining."

I was frightened. I was feeling a little stronger— Urban's mother had fattened me up on seafood gumbo down in Louisiana—and I didn't want to face another operation. The first time Bob set a date for me in surgery, I didn't show up. The next time, I went through with it. The operation lasted six and a half hours.

Dr. Brault dug deep into my intestine and found four slivers of wood, varying in length from two and a half to four and a half inches, each about an eighth of an inch in diameter. They were lodged in a muscle-and-scar-tissue area in the lower left quadrant of the abdomen. They'd been in there for twelve years. When I was seventeen, I'd been chasing a calf, and the calf had stepped on a plank of wood, and the plank had shot up into my groin. I had an operation then to have the splinters removed, but these four had escaped detection. They had caused the tumor on my liver; they had prevented me from healing.

Bob Brault and his assistants removed the splinters, resected the small intestine and the large intestine, and gave me four blood transfusions during the operation. Ten days later, I was playing golf. I still had to have two more operations, one to fix the colostomy and one to fix a hernia near the breastbone, but by the middle of July 1965, when training camp opened, I was able to start playing football again.

I was still pretty weak, still underweight, and for a while, I practiced with a hole in my stomach, an open, healing wound. It didn't bother me too much on the field, but I was a little hesitant to go into the shower with the rest of the guys. The hole in my stomach wasn't very pretty. In fact, it was kind of nauseating. One day, fairly early in training camp, I went into the shower and a rookie defensive back came in and took one look at my stomach and almost turned white.

"This is a rough game, kid," I said.

We all got a big laugh out of that.

By the middle of the 1965 season, I was back in the starting lineup, back up to my normal playing weight; everything in the world seemed beautiful to me. Not only did I feel almost completely healthy for the first time in more than a year, but I was moving perceptibly toward my goal of financial independence. The diving company was starting to make a little money in Mexico, and Urban, who'd been injured while playing for the Pittsburgh Steelers, had gone home to Morgan City and had opened a Louisiana branch of the Packer Diving Company.

At the beginning, the heart of the diving operation remained in Mexico, but in the next three years, as Urban committed himself totally to the success of the business, and as I devoted part of my off-season to building up contacts with oil companies, drumming up diving contracts, the balance shifted. By 1968, we were grossing more than $250,000 annually in Mexico and $1 million annually in Morgan City.

It felt good to be a successful businessman. I had felt so bad physically when I had first decided to dedicate myself to financial independence, when I had realized that I might never play football again, and now I felt that I had really accomplished something. If you work hard enough, you can be what you want to be. You can do what you want to do.

In 1969, we were offered $2 million for the diving company Urban Henry, Sam Mutrux, and I had started for $5,000 apiece. I had come a long way from making $4.60 a month.

I had come a long way, too, from a western childhood of hand-me-down clothes and homemade root beer.

4

Coming of Age

WHEN I ENTERED Farmin Junior High in Sandpoint, Idaho, the seventh grade was divided into three divisions: 7-1 for the smart students, 7-2 for the medium students, and 7-3 for the dummies. I didn't know anything about the divisions when I got to the school, and one of the kids asked me, "What are you in—seven-one, seven-two, or seven-three?"

"I'm in the seventh grade," I said.

"Which one?" He explained the three divisions to me.

"Where's seven-two?" I said. "I'm normal."

I entered the 7-2 classroom, and I looked at the names on the board, and my name wasn't there. "Oh, my God," I thought, "I'm a dummy."

I guess you could say that when I was growing up, I wasn't exactly filled with overconfidence. My immediate reaction was to go to 7-3. I didn't think I was a good student. I didn't think I was a good athlete, either; I was so clumsy I could hardly walk and chew gum at the same time.

As it turned out, I suppose I was pessimistic on both counts. When I got to 7-3, I found my name wasn't on the board there. I actually belonged in 7-1. The next year, I kept my grades up and I was in 8-1. We had an excellent intramural athletic program, and for the football championship, 8-1 played 8-3, the brains vs. the jocks. I played end for 8-1, and I caught a long pass, looking back over my shoulder, for the only touchdown in the game, and the brains beat the jocks 7–0. I certainly wasn't the smartest kid in school, and I certainly wasn't the most athletic, but I may have been either the strongest brain or the smartest jock.

I look back on those days now, and I miss them. I miss the thrill of accomplishing something for the first time, of enjoying unexpected victory for the first time. Our 8-1 team won the softball championship as well as the football championship, and I think it was that final softball game that first made me realize the value of motivation. We were playing 8-3 again, and they really had a much stronger team. But we wanted to win; we wanted to win very badly. We had kids with thick glasses who couldn't even see the ball who were catching it and hitting it that day. I remember one boy in particular, Freddy Rasp, a fine student, a brilliant science mind, an excellent mathematician. But he had miserable eyes and no co-ordination. I remember him circling and staggering under a fly ball, straining until he caught it for the final out that saved the game.

I had a good childhood, a beautiful childhood, a lot like a million other childhoods, I imagine, except maybe I was a bit more accident prone than most. We didn't have too much money most of the time, and we didn't have all the material things, and I was so reckless I almost got myself killed half a dozen times, but looking back now, I've got no major complaints. I've got a few little complaints. I suppose my mother didn't have to keep telling me, "Now, Gerald, do the right thing, always do the right thing," and I suppose my father didn't have to use the razor strop quite so often, unless he was just trying to toughen me up for Lombardi, and I know my older brother Russ didn't have to beat up on me so many times. But I learned manners from my mother, and I learned discipline from my father, and I learned sturdiness from my brother, and from all of them, and from all the people around us, I learned to love small pleasures, basic joys, like a frosty snow or a leaping trout. I went through childhood with a combination of innocence and enthusiasm that seems so rare today.

I was born in Jordan, Montana, on January 23, 1936, the fourth of six children, the second of two sons. I still hear stories about the hard times in Montana, the terribly severe winters—my father worked on the WPA for a while—but I don't remember suffering. I guess it's appropriate that the first thing I recall clearly was almost cutting my head off with an axe. I was about three years old, and I went out to help my mother chop some wood. I wanted to be a big shot and I picked up a big axe and held it over my head and it threw me off balance and I dropped it and then I fell on it. I cut my chin and cut my throat, and I got a bunch of stitches, but it was just on the surface, not anything serious.

We left Jordan before I was old enough to start school, but I've got a vivid memory of going one day with Russ. They had a visitors' day at his school, and I got up very early and got all cleaned up, and I wore one of Russ's shirts. All through childhood, into high school, I wore Russ's old clothes. I almost never had any new clothes of my own. I remember once, later on, maybe in the seventh grade, I had a new shirt my mother had bought me at J. C. Penney, and

I wore it to school, and one kid asked me where my shirt was from. He was wearing an Arrow shirt, and he made me show him the label on my shirt, and when he saw it was from J. C. Penney, he started making fun of me. He made me feel miserable, and I swore I'd never wear anything from J. C. Penney again.

Today I've got a real weakness for clothes. I'll buy a dozen sweaters or ten pairs of slacks at a time, the best I can buy, and I suppose it all dates back to then, when I wore hand-me-downs and got in the habit of rolling up the sleeves of my shirts so they wouldn't hang down to my feet. Now I've got more clothes than I can possibly wear, more than anyone needs; the guys on the Packers were always needling me, asking me when I was going to have a rummage sale so that they could buy the clothes I hadn't worn yet.

When I got to school with Russ, I got scared and didn't want to go into the classroom. Russ coaxed me in, and finally I entered, and the boy who normally sat next to him was absent, so I sat in that seat. I had a great day in school; I really enjoyed it. The next morning, I popped up early again and put on the same clothes and trotted off to school with Russ. The teacher wasn't too happy. She told Russ that once was all right, but I was getting to be a pest. She let me stay in school till noon, then sent me home.

I was so happy and proud that I'd spent a day and a half in school. I suppose lots of kids get off to a bad start in school and don't like it, but I was lucky. I liked school right from the first experience, always liked it, always liked learning. And this has carried over, too, to today. I meet someone and I want to know all about him and about what he does. I met Norman Mailer, the writer, at a party once, and I was awed and impressed and curious, but I just couldn't figure him out. He started using a thick southern drawl, puffing out his chest and talking like a sheriff in a movie, and I was a little insecure; I thought he was making fun of me. Later, I was told this was Mailer's way of showing he liked me. One night before a game in 1968, I met Flip Wilson, the comedian, and I sat with him for several hours, listening to him explain his theories of comedy. I'd never realized how hard he had to work, how thoroughly he had to be prepared, in order to appear totally casual and relaxed. I met Frank Sinatra at one of his recording sessions, and I was fascinated by him, by his style, by his technique. I think I'd really like to know everything about everything. I'd like to be able to do everything—to fly a plane and ride a rocket into orbit. I love every new experience.

When I turned six, we moved from Jordan to Salt Lake City, and, financially, things were better there. My father worked at Hill Field Air Force Base, working in electronics, on radio equipment and things like that. He hadn't gone to college—no one else in my family went to college—but he had a good mind, picked things up very quickly, and studied hard at his field. He really had a fine mind for electronics. When I was in the third grade, he helped me build my own radio.

My mother worked at the air base too. Russ used to go out there with her occasionally, and a group of Italian prisoners of war taught him how to swear in Italian. After six months in Salt Lake City, we moved out about twenty miles to a government housing project in Layton, Utah. For three years, we lived in house number 11 on court G in the government project.

Layton was fun. We had our own bottle-capping machine and we made our own root beer in the basement. I even had a dollar a week allowance for about two weeks. The first dollar I ever received was a silver dollar. I dropped it down a crack next to a window and never saw it again. I started a butterfly collection, and once I caught a huge yellow butterfly, the prize of my collection, and I called it my secret butterfly. We had good Christmases and good family picnics and good fishing trips. Dad and Russ and I would go up to Weaver Canyon and bring back a gunny sack full of fresh-water suckers and hand them out to all the neighbors. The fish must have been spawning up in the clear mountain streams, they were so thick. I had a terrible time trying to hook them, so sometimes I just jumped in the water and cornered the fish in the rocks and grabbed them with my hands, nice-sized fish, some of them twelve and fourteen inches long.

My strongest memory of school in Layton isn't a pleasant one, but it wasn't bad enough to turn me against school. We were coloring one day, in the first grade, I think, and I lost my blue crayon. Nobody'd lend me a blue crayon to color the sky in my drawing. I had to color my sky purple, and all the other kids laughed at me for coloring the sky purple. They hurt me. I've seen purple skies since then, and I've wished that all the kids who were in my class at Layton could've seen those purple skies with me.

I don't know if that incident with the blue crayon spurred me or not, but I became pretty competitive in school in Layton. In the third grade, I was the best in the class in arithmetic. The teacher always used to say, "All right, let's see if we can beat Gerald today." I always finished first.

Naturally, I had a few brushes with disaster in Layton, just like everywhere else. Sometimes I think my whole childhood was a series of accidents, mostly major ones, but they never seemed to dampen my spirit or make me any more cautious. In Layton, I went on a picnic once with my mother—my father'd gone off on a trip, some air force work—and I climbed up in a tree, and a dry limb broke. I tumbled down and cut up my arm pretty bad. I needed six or seven stitches, and the doctor didn't have any anesthetic. He had a hard time penetrating my skin; he had to change needles twice. "Don't cry," he said, and I didn't. My mother wrote my father a letter—he still has it—saying not how brave I was, but how tough my skin was. I guess I started getting used to pain at a very early age, and it never seemed to bother me as much as most kids. Once in a while, I wonder if it's just a case of "No brain, no pain."

I do come from a sturdy line of people. My dad's six foot five, and he's got a younger brother, Uncle Bud, who's six foot eight. Bud's a cowboy, a rancher in Montana, and I haven't seen him since I was about six years old, but I remember in his cowboy boots and his stetson he looked like he was eight feet tall. And my mother's father, Grandpa Reddy, was strong as a bull even when he was about sixty years old. He was limber and active as hell. He'd come into a room and he'd step over furniture, not around it.

My little son, Danny, seems to have inherited some of my resistance to pain. He jumped off a barn not long after his fourth birthday and banged his leg pretty good. He just bawled for about three minutes, then jumped up and ran off into the woods, playing with our dogs. After half an hour, I began to worry about him. I called the dogs, and when they showed up, I set out in the direction they'd come from. I finally found Danny deep in the woods, where he knew he wasn't supposed to go. I got a switch and blistered his butt, four or five real good smacks, but when we got back to the house, he was giggling. I'd hurt his feelings more than I'd hurt him.

I'd always played where I wasn't supposed to play, too. In Layton, all of us kids used to fool around in little irrigation ditches, two feet deep and maybe three feet wide. We'd sit on a board, and the current was pretty swift, and we'd ride down the irrigation ditch.

One time my father bought me a brand new pair of Levi's, and I went right out to the irrigation ditch and wore a hole in the seat. When I got home, my father tried to wear a hole in my seat. He didn't believe in spoiling the child at all.

I believe in spanking a child, too, and I believe in spanking him in anger. I don't believe in waiting till tomorrow and thinking it all out and patting his butt. Yet I probably haven't spanked my children more than five times each in their lives. I didn't paddle Danny when he started the fire that burned down our house. I didn't want him to have any permanent psychological scar from the accident, but I did want him to realize what he'd done. Barbara told me Danny hadn't cried at all at the time of the fire, but later I took him to the burned-out house and showed him the charred furniture from his room and his melted toys and I sat him down. "Dan," I said, "I've got to talk to you about this. I want you to understand what can happen from playing with matches." He burst into tears and he cried for a long time. I don't know whether I handled the situation right or not. I hope so. I once started a house fire myself, when I was a child in Jordan—the firemen came and put out the blaze before there was any real damage—and I know how the memory stays with you.

When I was seven, close to eight, my brother Russ decided he was going to teach me how to swim in a big irrigation ditch, twenty feet wide and ten or twenty feet deep. I sort of asked for it. We'd been out to one of the lakes, and I'd been crying about not being allowed to swim.

"I'll teach you," Russ said.

He threw me in the ditch.

I didn't have the slightest idea how to swim. I thrashed my arms around, and I started to sink. Russ reached over and grabbed my chin and pulled me up a little, and then I started to sink again. We were on one side of a highway, and the ditch disappeared under the highway into a huge metal culvert, maybe six or eight feet in diameter, then came out the other side of the highway in a big pipe that carried the water all the way down the valley for miles and miles. I was starting to sink, sliding toward the culvert, and I have a distinct recollection of swaying. The banks of the ditch were swaying, and I was swaying, and the whole feeling was very peaceful, very calm, and then Russ leaned down and grabbed me by the hair. He pulled me out by the hair, or I would have gone into the culvert and gone miles and miles, and it would have been all over.

Russ told me that he'd beat me up if I told the old man what had happened. I think, just to make sure I didn't tell anyone, Russ beat me up anyway. He didn't really hurt me; he just whacked me a few times, sort of pressured me. One time I caught him smoking—he must've been about twelve or thirteen —and I said, "I'm going to tell the old man." I was only teasing, but Russ whipped me pretty good. Another time, in Layton, he and I were supposed to rake the yard, but I ran off to play and left him alone. When I came back, he had the whole yard raked. "Come on in the house," Russ said. "I want to talk to you."

I wasn't that dumb. "No deal," I said.

He ran out and caught me on the lawn and blacked my eye and bloodied my lip. A neighbor lady came by and told Russ to stop killing me.

I don't want to give the wrong impression; Russ was a good brother. I was closer to him than I was to either of my parents. Later, when I played in that eighth-grade football game, he let me wear his cleats. He'd played halfback on the Sandpoint High School team, and he'd been an excellent runner, a much better prospect than I ever was, according to coach Cotton Barlow. Russ quit high school before he graduated, so he never had a chance to prove how good he was.

He always helped me out. Once, when I was in my early teens, I was taking a girl to the movies. The show cost twelve cents each at the time, and I asked my father for the money. He gave me a quarter. "Son," he said, "that's plenty to get into the show, but not much good for Cokes or popcorn or any of that good stuff." I asked him for an extra dime, but he wouldn't give it to me, either because he didn't have it or he just didn't want to give it to me. Russ came up with fifty cents for me. He had a dollar or a dollar and a half, and he gave me fifty cents. He'd always do things like that. If he had only forty cents, he'd give me a dime. He lives up in Alaska now and works on construction and hunts a lot, but we're still very close. I've been able to help him out in business a little, not very much, but if he asked me for my house and my car and my farm, I'd give them to him, simple as that. I don't believe I could ever turn Russ down on anything, he was so good to me.

We came close to a fight once, when I was big enough to fight him. I was a sophomore in college, and I came home from school one weekend, and we went out to a party. Russ drank quite a bit that night, and I was still pretty much an orange-pop man. After the party, he wanted to drive, and I said, "No, I'm driving," and I climbed in the driver's seat. He slammed the door on my leg and started laughing and giggling and wouldn't let my leg go.

I finally shoved the door open, pushed Russ down, and jumped out of the car, really angry. "Come on," he said, sticking out his chin, "I'll spot you the first one." I wouldn't hit him first, he wouldn't hit me first, so we started wrestling. We rolled over five acres, and I kept thinking about how Russ'd always helped me, and when we ended up down by the lake, both of us were crying, actually bawling. "I couldn't hit you," Russ said.

"You're my brother. You know I wasn't going to hit you. I couldn't hit you." We were both crying at the thought that we'd even come close to hurting each other.

On V-J Day, in August 1945, we left Layton and moved to Sandpoint, Idaho. I can't think of a more beautiful place for a boy to grow up. Sandpoint is in the high country of Idaho, some twenty-five hundred or three thousand feet above sea level, nestled in mountains and tremendous pine forests, on the shores of Lake Pend Oreille, where the world's largest rainbow trout—37 pounds, 10 ounces, I think—was caught. There's a ski hill just out of town, and a golf course, and the air is clean and pure as a mountain stream.

The population of Sandpoint was about four or five thousand when I was growing up there, and it hasn't changed much since. I got to know every street in the town and most of the people, and they were good people. I always had the feeling that there were a lot of capable people in Sandpoint, who could have really done well somewhere else, but they deliberately chose the life of Sandpoint. They liked the pace. They loved something like Howdy Week, the opening week of the fishing season on Lake Pend Oreille. I remember once going out on a houseboat during Howdy Week and sitting in a big captain's chair and trolling across the lake and watching the sun set, an incredibly gorgeous sunset. I hated for that moment to end. I hated for the day to be over, it was so beautiful.

I must've been a little big for my age when I got to Idaho, but I wasn't big enough. The older boys were always setting me up, possibly because I was such a good marble player—I had a great eye—and I'd won a lot of marbles from them. I remember one kid egging me on in the schoolyard, saying, "Kramer, I bet you're scared to go down the slide backward. Bet you're scared."

"No, I'm not, either," I said. I started sliding down

backward, and the other kid yelled, "Hey, teacher, Kramer's going down the slide backward." She grabbed me and marched me off to the principal's office, and I got paddled. Guess I wasn't too bright.

The next year, when I was in fifth grade, some of the kids in sixth grade asked me if I wanted to play tackle football. I didn't know anything about football, so they explained the game to me. "You get the ball and you try to go from here to there," they said, "and you can't step outside these lines. You have to run up the middle." They gave me the ball to carry every play, and they must have been setting me up, because they cut my lip and my nose, and I had to go to the principal's office and get some bandages and clean myself up. I learned a lot that day. From then on, either I didn't run up the middle, or I stayed in the line and got to hit someone else.

I fell madly in love for the first time in the fourth grade. Her name was Maxine, and she lived in a house in the mountains. I used to walk eight miles to get there, then just stand outside her house and moon around. She liked me, too, but she didn't always show it very well. One day she looked out her window and saw me and said, "Get out of here, you little sonuvabitch."

Maxine was ten at the time. I guess she'd heard somebody say that, and she was just repeating it. It made me feel kind of funny, but she was still my girl friend through the sixth grade.

For the first few years in Sandpoint, we didn't have much money. We always had enough to eat, but there wasn't anything left over for luxuries. Dad opened his own shop, a tiny radio shop in half of a little second-hand store. Dad worked like hell, twelve and fifteen hours a day, building up his business, and, eventually, he had a damn fine business, radio and television and all kinds of appliances, with ten or fifteen employees and four or five pickup trucks. But at the beginning, he had to scramble.

I didn't get to see Dad too much in those days. We didn't have a car for a few years, and he walked a little over two miles each way to and from his shop. He'd leave the house about seven in the morning and wouldn't get home until nine or ten at night. For a while, the only time I'd see him was when I'd done something wrong, when I was going to get my butt whipped. Instead of any closeness between us, an ill-feeling developed. I began to look upon him as just a disciplinarian.

Once, when I was about eleven or twelve, Dad asked me to watch the shop while he went out on a call. While he was gone, I stole fifty cents out of the till. I figured he'd whip me, but I'd had my butt whipped a lot and it didn't mean that much any more. That evening, when he got home, he walked up to me and said, "Were you messing with that till?"

"Nope," I said.

"Were you messing with that till?" he repeated.

"No," I said. "I wasn't."

"I'm four bits short," Dad said, "and somebody was messing with the till."

I couldn't lie any more. "I took it," I said. I was ready for my whipping. I just wanted him to get it over with.

Dad stared at me for a long time and, finally, he said, "Son, if I can't trust you, who can I trust?"

And he turned and he walked out of the house, and I felt absolutely miserable. I was ready to take a beating, but I wasn't ready to take that.

I looked at my father differently from then on. I really wanted to please him. I wanted to make him trust me and like me. But, still, it took a long time for us to get close. It didn't really happen, I suppose, until I left for college. Dad had more free time then, and maybe he realized he was going to miss me, and I realized I was going to miss him, and we've been close ever since, hunting and fishing and golfing whenever we can.

I'm sure it's because my father was so busy that I worry now about finding enough time to spend with my three children. I like to be with each of them alone every now and then, a trip to the store with Tony, the oldest, or a lunch with Danny, the youngest, or a dinner with Diane. They're all competing for my attention, of course, and I want to make sure that each of them gets some individual attention. I want to share their fun with all of them.

In Idaho, we had some good family times in the winter, when we'd get snowbound and Dad couldn't get to work. We had one huge blizzard in 1948, when I was twelve, and we had to spend several days in the house, the temperature outside running twenty-five and thirty-five degrees below zero. My father and my brother and I would stay up all night in the kitchen, with the stove on, first playing pinochle—till Dad and Russ got disgusted with my bad playing—then playing Monopoly. Dad would find time then to read to us, poems and stories and especially Robert Service, the Canadian poet who wrote about Alaska. I've loved poetry ever since, all kinds of poetry, ranging from Wallace Stevens to my friend Rod McKuen. My mother was always very poetic about birds and flowers, and she taught me to appreciate the beauty in life. I read everything I could get my hands on, the Wizard of Oz books, the Albert Payson Terhune dog books, all the horse books. Nobody else in my family cared that much about reading, but I just couldn't get enough of it. In school, I'd walk from class to class reading a book.

My mother and father both taught Sunday school in Sandpoint, and, naturally, churchgoing was a ritual. Every Sunday morning, we hit the deck automatically,

Russ and I and my older sisters Kiki and Barbara and my younger sisters Martha and Carol, all of us scrubbed and polished and off to church. It was an absolute requirement, no questions about it. There were always a lot of things I'd rather be doing, like fishing or playing with the other kids, but I always ended up spending the whole morning in church, going to services and to Sunday school. I remember one Sunday-school teacher I really liked. We called him Uncle Bob, and he wasn't one of those beat-it-into-your-head, sit-up-straight, don't-wiggle-or-God'll-get-you types. He discussed things with us on an open, friendly basis. He'd read something out of the Bible and he'd say, "Well, Jerry, what do you think about this?" And he cared what I thought.

We changed churches a few times, from Lutheran to Methodist to, finally, the Church of the Nazarene, but, always, my folks stressed the importance of religion, of living the proper life. The church dominated our lives on Sundays. Sometimes we'd go to a church social in the afternoon, with everybody bringing a different dish and the kids playing run-sheep-run and kick-the-can and red light-green light, and then we'd go back to services in the evening.

Occasionally, we'd go to a neighbor's for a dress-up Sunday dinner after church, and I really had to behave then. My father's theory was that either you sat up straight and minded your manners or you paid the consequences. And Mom always reminded me, "I want you to eat everything on your plate." Once—I think it was when I was only five or six, before we moved to Idaho—I had a big, green onion on my plate, and I could barely look at it. But I chewed it all up. When I finished, I looked down at my plate, and there was another green onion. I was sure Russ had snuck his onion onto my plate, but years later my sister Kiki confessed she had done it.

I remember running away from home not long after

we'd moved to Sandpoint. I'd had a fight with Mom, and I'd decided that was it. I was leaving forever. I got a half a mile away and discovered a little stream filled with fish. I turned around, went home, got my fishing pole, and I forgot all about running away. For the next eight or ten years, I fished that stream.

The more I look back, the more it strikes me I had almost a perfect childhood, a good blend of fun and strictness and learning and hard work, not a thing that would ever hurt me. During summers, I often worked for Grandpa Reddy. I was his go-for, running odd errands for him. He'd get me out to his little farm —he liked to speculate in cattle—about six or seven in the morning, and he'd run me all day long and give me fifty cents a day. I had the normal paper route, too, in the sixth grade and in junior high, getting up about four in the morning and delivering the Spokane paper in pitch-black darkness. Once we had a big freeze and I delivered the papers on skates for three hours, and my ankles were stiff for a whole week afterward.

Yet I wasn't exactly a little saint. When I got into junior high, I ran around briefly with a bunch of wild kids. We were into all kinds of trouble, shooting out windows and rifling jockey boxes, the glove compartments of cars. Two or three times, I got into trouble with the police, and the last time, they were going to throw the book at me, to put me on probation and get me suspended from school. Then Charlie Stidwell, the principal of Farmin Junior High, stepped in and helped me get straightened out. He went to the police and persuaded them to let me go. He was one of the first people outside my own family to take a real interest in me, to show me that I might have some future outside Sandpoint.

Charlie Stidwell was a teacher, as well as the principal, and he took a tremendous interest in all his kids. Perhaps because he was a bachelor and had no children of his own, he treated each of his students as if they were his own kids. We used to go up to his house, half a dozen of us at a time, and pop popcorn and sit around and talk. When I'd get in trouble with my homeroom teacher, she'd send me to Charlie Stidwell's office. He'd yell at me a little and scare me and then say, "Go get my mail." He'd throw me the key to his mail box, which was about three blocks away. Then he'd throw me a dime and say, "And get yourself an ice cream cone along the way." He was a good guy, a rare person. All through my life, I've been very fortunate in coming across people like Charlie Stidwell, people who would help me and encourage me. I've been down on myself so many times, completely discouraged, and somebody has always come along to pull me up by the bootstraps.

My first year in high school, I went out for football and made the freshman team. I wasn't exactly a big star; if someone had suggested then that I might be an All-Pro football player in ten years, everybody would have laughed at him. I'd have laughed, too. I was a gangly kid—my coach called me "Slim"—and still not too well co-ordinated. I played end on the freshman team, and I caught a grand total of one pass all year, a pass that somebody else deflected. The ball wobbled in the air, and I caught it for a one-yard gain. The freshmen played only three or four games, and at the end of our short season, the best players were promoted to the varsity. Two of my closest friends, George Kom and Roger Olson, were picked for the varsity, but I wasn't. I wasn't really surprised, but I was kind of disappointed and embarrassed. It would have been a tremendous thrill for me just to get into a varsity game.

The next year, I played on the varsity. Coach Cotton Barlow switched me to tackle—I guess he'd really been impressed by my quick pass-catching hands—and halfway through the season, somebody got hurt and I moved into the starting lineup. I enjoyed one of my typical little mishaps during the season. The day of a night game, I was working in shop class, building a lamp, and I dropped a piece of sandpaper. When I bent over to pick it up, the turning screw of the lathe caught my T shirt and pulled me into the lathe and ripped out a fist-sized chunk of my right side. The shop teacher hustled me to the clinic, and the doctor came and put eight or ten stitches in my hide. Coach Barlow came by the clinic and said, "I don't suppose there's any chance of him playing tonight, just kicking off."

"I guess he can kick off," the doctor said, "as long as he doesn't make any tackles."

I kicked off to start the game and ran down the field as fast as I could and made the tackle and ripped out the stitches and bled most of the night.

Two things happened during that sophomore year that definitely influenced my future. First, a coach from the University of Idaho came to our dressing room to talk to a few of our seniors. I was sitting on a bench, and he walked over to me and patted me on the head and said, "You're the kind of boy we want to have at the University of Idaho one of these days."

For the first time, I began to think about going to college. I was really flattered by the coach's interest, and I started day-dreaming about college, about studying engineering, stuff like that. I was so excited about the possibility of going to college that I ran home to tell my father.

My father sort of mumbled when I told him, and he said, "I'd like to see you go to M.I.T."

"What's M.I.T.?" I said. "Where's that?"

"It's in Massachusetts," Dad said. "It's the Massachusetts Institute of Technology, and it's a great school for engineering."

I was taking all the math courses and all the science courses I could, but M.I.T. was just too remote a possibility for me to accept. The University of Idaho was a big enough dream for me.

About the same time, Dusty Klein, who was an assistant coach under Cotton Barlow, made a comment to me about the size of my hands. No one had ever told me before that I was a little different or unusual, and I didn't know what it meant to have big hands, but Dusty Klein said, "Son, you're going to be a good football player. You've got big hands."

The combination of the Idaho coach's remark and Dusty Klein's remark got me thinking that maybe I was something special, that maybe I could do something with football and with my life that'd set me apart a little. We all had our little dreams about being rich someday. In Sandpoint, being rich meant having a new Ford and a new rifle and maybe a house with a fireplace. Taking a trip to Detroit or Chicago or New York was Alice-in-Wonderland stuff, almost beyond our imagination. The real extreme, fantastic wealth, was to have a Chriscraft Century, a 100-horsepower outboard. Cabin cruisers were inconceivable. I drive around now in my big Lincoln Continental, with its telephone and its stereo, and I sometimes wish I still had the old dreams.

We had one pro football player that I knew of from Sandpoint, a fellow named Kennedy, and not long after Dusty Klein's comment, I met Kennedy in a local saloon—I'd snuck in to bang on the pinball machines—and he noticed my hands, too. I was sixteen then, about 170 pounds and a little over six feet tall, but Kennedy said that my hands meant that I was going to fill out, that I was going to be a big, strong boy.

By my junior year, I was up to six foot two and 195 pounds, and I wanted to play in the backfield. I wanted the glory of carrying the ball. "Look," coach Barlow told me, "George Kom's our fullback, and he's a good one. If you want to play in the backfield, you can be a second-string fullback. But if you stay in the line, you can be a real good lineman." I stayed at tackle, playing both offense and defense, doing all our place-kicking. I had a good year, but I wasn't really a star. I never did think of myself as a star in high school; I guess I always had that lineman's inferiority complex.

The week before our final game of the 1952 season, George Kom and I went duck-hunting. George was out in a rowboat, circling around, and I was on the shore, sitting on a huge rock. I was just fooling around, aiming at ducks and geese too far away to hit, enjoying a bright November sun. The rock was about two stories high, with moss growing all over it. I kept scooping up pieces of moss, working them into a ball, and rolling them down the rock into the water. One ball of moss started rolling, then stopped by my foot. I grabbed the barrel of my grandfather's old double-barrel 10-gauge shotgun and, with the butt of the gun, jabbed at the ball of moss.

I couldn't believe it. The gun went off.

I still don't recall hearing any sound, but I felt a terrible shock, a numbing concussion shock. Then I saw the blood spurting out of my right arm like it was coming out of a hose. The blood shot out six, eight feet, a thick, red arterial stream. Steam rose off the rock—the shotgun had slipped into the water—and blood was everywhere, and I kept thinking, "It can't be, it just can't be."

I looked at my arm, and it looked like hamburger. Everything was blown back into a big ball, flesh, tendons, muscles, everything. I screamed. I screamed for George to come help me. By the time he'd rowed ashore, I'd walked about two hundred yards across a field toward a farmhouse. "You all right?" he said, when he caught up with me.

"No, I'm not all right," I said. I couldn't touch my arm—it was in complete shock—but I was clutching my side. I'd caught fifteen or twenty pellets of No. 2 shot, pretty good-sized shot, in my side, and it burned like hell. I looked down at my pants and I couldn't see a single dry spot, not one spot where there wasn't blood. I told George I was getting weak and tired and I had to lie down. He ran ahead and found a fellow named Dan Chaney, who put me in the back seat of his car and drove me to Bonner County General Hospital in Sandpoint, about four miles away. I moaned all the way.

When we got to the hospital, I walked out of the car myself and into the emergency room, and the nurse on duty took one look at me and almost passed out. They put me right on the operating table and gave me a shot to knock me out. My parents rushed to the hospital. The word must have spread pretty fast because, while I was unconscious—I heard later—my youngest sister, Carol, ran over to a neighbor's house, shouting, "Jerry's shot, but he's not dead yet." I guess that's the way the whole family felt about me during all my accidents: He's not dead yet. Incidentally, our address at the time was 1313 Chestnut, which may explain something.

Three local physicians, Bill Hayden and Neil Wendle and J. P. Munson, worked on me, and they did a beautiful job. They must have operated at least three or four times, delicately repairing the nerves and the tendons, pulling out all the clothing that had been blown into my arm. I've been told several times since by specialists that those Sandpoint general practitioners did a fantastic job in saving my arm.

At one point, a threat of gangrene existed, and the doctors actually drew a line across my right arm just below the elbow. It scared the hell out of me. It was the only thing about the whole episode that really terrified me. I didn't want to lose the arm no matter what.

The doctors, after consulting with my parents, decided not to amputate, but I needed skin grafts, from my leg to my arm, and I needed a great deal of blood. My mother gave a pint, my brother gave a pint, and so did a few townspeople, including Don Samuelson, who was then running a sporting goods store in Sandpoint and later became Governor of Idaho.

For several days, the most excruciating pain was a redhot burning in the palm of my right hand, caused by the damage to the nerves in my arm.

My nurse was the mother of Kenny Armstrong, one of my teammates, and she took good care of me, cheering me up and teaching me how to play cribbage. I guess I ought to give her a percentage of all the money I later won playing cribbage in the Green Bay Packers training camp. Once I started feeling better in the hospital, Kenny's mother and I played practical jokes on each other. I'd soak my thermometer in hot water and bring the temperature up to 105; she'd bake me an apple pie with red-hot pepper in it, and she'd pour salt in the bottom of my milk glass.

Four days after my accident, Sandpoint played Bonners Ferry, and I listened on the radio, and Art Miller and Bill Davis, our co-captains, got on the air and said they were playing the game for me. They beat Bonners Ferry 45–0, and everybody signed the game ball and gave it to me. It was a tough way to get my first game ball.

The following week, the football players got together and sponsored a Gerald Kramer Benefit Dance at the Elks Temple. It was a beautiful thing for them to do. They raised enough money to pay my hospital bills.

While I was recuperating in the hospital, my dog died. He was a Chesapeake named Sandy, and I'd had him for seven or eight years. He was a wonderful animal, more human than he was dog. He used to take care of all us children; he wouldn't let anybody come near us when we were sleeping. Even if our folks tried to wake us up in the morning, Sandy would chew on their feet to keep them away. Once I was sleeping out in the backyard and my boss on the paper route came to wake me up. Sandy wouldn't let him get close to me. He tried to poke me with a long stick, and Sandy kept pushing the stick away. I woke up, eventually, but I didn't move. I just lay there, giggling to myself, watching Sandy protect me, until my boss saw that I was giggling and started cussing me out.

When I heard that Sandy had died, I asked my mother not to do anything with him till I got home. I was out of the hospital ten days after the accident, a remarkably quick recovery, according to the doctors, and the first thing I did was dig a grave for Sandy. With my bad arm and my leg aching from the skin grafts, I couldn't work very well. It took me three hours to dig Sandy's grave.

The next thing I did was go out with my father and buy a new shotgun. I wasn't about to give up hunting just because of a slight mistake.

The arm felt like cloth for almost a year. At first, I couldn't move the fingers and I could barely wiggle the thumb, but I exercised with a rubber ball and I took whirlpool treatments and had more skin grafts and underwent plastic surgery. Several times over the next few years, surgeons cut underneath the scarred skin and pulled it forward and tightened it up and removed some of the remaining scar tissue. Little by little, I got my strength back.

Shortly after the hospital released me, we had our annual football banquet at a nice restaurant out on Lake Pend Oreille. I must've looked pretty terrible limping into the banquet. Because of the skin grafts, my legs were all bandaged up and hurting, and I had to walk kind of stiff-legged. The guest speaker was the University of Idaho coach who'd patted me on the head when I was a sophomore, who'd said such encouraging things to me, and I was very much looking forward to seeing him again. He didn't pay any attention to me. He didn't say a word to me. I suppose he must've seen a million high school kids, and I certainly didn't look like a prize prospect, but I was really hurt by his slight. I swore to myself that I'd show him, that I'd become a great football player and that I'd never go to the University of Idaho. Of course, I did end up going to the University, but by that time, he had lost his job.

I missed the basketball season my junior year, but I came back for track and field, putting the shot and throwing the discus. Then, in July, between my junior and senior years, I did it again. I had another near-fatal accident.

Roger Olson and I went swimming one afternoon. Roger was a good friend, a football and basketball teammate, and in my senior year, I beat him in the voting for the best-looking boy in school; actually, I've got to admit Roger was better looking, but some of the kids voting thought he was a little stuck-up. Roger and I decided that we were going to keep swimming at night. He said he'd wait for me while I went home to milk the cow we kept in a pasture about three blocks from our house. When I got to the pasture, the cow's calf was running around loose. I had to catch him and tie him up, and I tried to do it quickly because I wanted to get back to the swimming.

First, I tried to lasso the calf with a little piece of cotton clothesline, but I couldn't even get close to him. Then I decided I'd chase him and grab hold of his tail and either throw him down or slip the rope around his neck. I cornered the calf next to the woodpile and, just as I was easing in on him, he bolted and dashed away. I took off after him as fast as I could, and, running through the pasture, he stepped on a board about ten feet long and one inch thick. He splintered the board, and the sharp end of one half flew up in the air. The flat end was firm against the ground. Running at top speed, I raced smack into the sharp end. It sank deep into my groin.

I lay down and pried myself loose and started hollering for my father. He came running from the house—my yells carried that far—looked at me and said, "Don't move, don't do anything." Dad went and called my doctor, but he was out of town, so Dad had to find another, and I lay there for forty-five minutes before the doctor arrived in a little black car.

He took me to the hospital, and I had to suffer through a terribly uncomfortable examination. The doctor put his finger in the hole that the stick had left. He told me that inside the hole he could actually feel the pumping of the large artery that runs into the leg. The sharp end of the board had come within the tiniest fraction of an inch of puncturing the artery. If it had hit the artery, I would've been dead by the time the doctor arrived.

As it was, I was hardly bleeding at all. But I was in agony. I couldn't straighten out my leg. I had to keep it in a bent position because, if I didn't, my back would hurt like hell. I lay in the hospital for a couple of days, my back killing me, and when my mother was visiting me, I said, "Mom, I think that thing went in six inches at least."

"No," she said, "it just went in a couple of inches."

"It went in at least six," I insisted.

The pain in my back kept getting worse and worse, and the X rays didn't show any logical explanation. X rays don't show wood. Finally, my own doctor went out to my house and pieced together the board that had cut me. He figured out that a part of the board was still missing, that when I'd pulled the sliver of wood out of me, I hadn't gotten all of it.

I was taken to a hospital in Spokane, and a team of doctors cut open my belly and went right through toward my back and found, lodged in a large muscle near the spine, perhaps half an inch short of coming out my back, a splinter seven and a half inches long and three-quarter of an inch thick. They removed the splinter. After the operation, I was wracked with gas pains—the doctors had taken out almost everything inside me to get to the splinter—and I spent probably the most miserably agonizing night of my life. But again, in ten days, I was out of the hospital. I hadn't learned a thing.

I started football practice about a week later, and it was absolute murder. I had no wind. I'd run two laps and I'd be down on my knees, gasping for breath. On Saturday night, after the first week of practice, I went out with a friend of mine, Glenn Oliver, who was about to start his freshman year at the University of Idaho. Glenn had a brand-new Cadillac—his folks were among the wealthier people in Sandpoint—and he wanted to show it off. We met a friend of my brother's, and he had my brother's car, and we decided we'd race to a tavern on the other side of town.

My brother's friend ran a red light and really raced through town. We took it fairly easy till we hit the outskirts, and then Glenn floorboarded it for about two miles. He had us moving 105 miles an hour, and we caught up to the other car, and Glenn started to pass. Just then, we reached the tavern we'd been aiming for, and the other car began to ease over to our side of the road. Glenn slammed the brakes, slid into the edge of a ditch, bounced out, hit the other car, knocked it off the road, banged up the front of the Cadillac, and started heading straight at a deep ditch on the other side of the road.

There was nothing we could do, no way to stop the Cadillac, no way to control it. We were still moving about seventy or eighty miles an hour, and we had to slide about seventy or eighty feet, and we just sat and waited for the crash. We had two, maybe three seconds, and it seemed like an eternity. Sometimes today, when I'm in a car and somebody else is driving and I fall asleep, I wake up suddenly and see that ditch in front of me and I grab the steering wheel. I bet I've done that not once or twice, but fifteen or twenty or thirty times. I'm lucky I haven't caused an accident.

We hit the ditch and we started rolling, sideways, not end over end. We rolled over once, twice, three times. Without even realizing it, I'd grabbed hold of the door handle, and all of a sudden, I looked up and I was in the bottom of the ditch, and a great mass of metal was rolling past me. Glenn fell out right after me, and fell on top of me and knocked all the wind out of me. I had nothing worse than the wind knocked out of me and a few scratches and a lot of gravel and dirt in my hair. The car rolled over two or three more times and hit a tree and burst into flames. Glenn jumped up and he wasn't hurt, either, and he started throwing gravel on his burning new car and yelling, "Get up and help me. Get up and help me. My car is burning." I knew his car was burning, but I couldn't get up. I had no wind at all.

One of the fellows in the other car had a broken back. The police came and took us downtown and checked us into the hospital, Bonner County General Hospital again, my favorite spot that year. The hospital just kept me for observation for a few hours this time and then sent me home.

On Monday, I was back at football practice. I still wasn't too strong, of course, and for the first game of the year, against St. Maries, a weak team, coach Cotton Barlow told me that I wasn't going to play and I wasn't going to kick off. I'd only kick extra points. When we went out on the field, my buddy, George Kom, found that he had forgotten his belt. I gave him mine. I didn't think I'd need it too much. We beat St. Maries 73–0, and we scored eleven touchdowns, and every time we scored, I ran out on the field, clutching my pants with one hand, and attempted the extra point.

I made seven extra points and I didn't drop my pants once.

The following week, we faced Moscow, and I played every single minute of the game. I was a little over six foot two then and weighed about 200 pounds. We won our first eight games by an average score of 35–7. Then we lost to Lewiston 13–7, which cost us the league championship. We finished up with a 9-1 record and placed three of our men on the Inland Empire all-league team. George Kom, our captain, made it at fullback, Kenny Armstrong made it at end, and I made it at tackle. I was happy, but I still didn't consider myself a big hero or anything. Coach Barlow called George Kom "the best player I've coached in fifteen years."

It's hard to believe, but I stayed healthy that whole year. (I never did have a major football injury all through high school and college.) I played the full basketball season, just a reserve, nothing special, and then I turned to track and field for the spring. I really concentrated on the shot-put, for one reason. My father had been a shot-putter when he was in high school, and he'd once told me that his best distance was about forty-four feet. I wanted to beat him.

My father never took too much of an interest in my athletic accomplishments in high school. He encouraged me in my schoolwork, but he didn't seem too impressed by sports. I wanted his approval very badly, and I thought maybe I could gain it by outdoing him in the shot-put. Early in my senior year, I threw the shot forty-five feet for the first time, and I rushed home to tell Dad, and he said, "Uh, huh, well, you'd better milk the cow." That was it.

Near the end of the track season, colleges began to take an interest in me, and I got an invitation to visit Washington State College. While I was there, Jack Mooberry, the Washington State track coach, took me aside and taught me the newest method of putting the shot, the Parry O'Brien method, in which you start facing directly opposite from the direction you're going to throw.

I went home and started practicing the O'Brien method, and I worked like hell on it. One day I stayed out late after practice, with a teammate named Marion Benton, a younger boy, who kept returning the shot to me. Marion was a good discus thrower, better than me, and he was just being nice and doing me a favor by helping me out with the shot. On one throw, he didn't realize I was getting ready to fire, and when I spun around and looked up, the shot was heading straight at Marion. I hollered. He looked up, and the shot caught him on the hairline, cut him open and fractured his skull. He had to go to the hospital. He wasn't seriously injured, but he was out of the district championships. I entered both the shot-put and the discus and won them both and gave the discus medal to Marion. He'd have won it anyway, if I hadn't hit him with the shot.

In the district meet, I put the shot forty-seven feet, seven inches, two feet beyond my best previous effort, an enormous improvement for a shot-putter. The next week, in the regional championships, after long, punishing hours of polishing my new technique, I threw forty-nine feet, nine inches, another two-foot gain. And then in the Idaho state track and field championships, I broke a record that had stood for twenty years. On my first try, I put the shot fifty-one feet, ten inches, five inches farther than any Idaho high school student had ever thrown. I was tremendously excited; I'd improved six feet in less than a month. I went home afterward and said to my father, "Dad, I broke . . ." He cut me off and said, "Yeah, I heard about it."

That was just about the end of my high school days, the end of living full time in Sandpoint, the end, I guess, of my childhood. I'd come through scarred but alive, and it seemed like I'd traveled a long distance, from utter clumsiness in sports to all-league in football and a state record in the shot-put, from an uncertain kid, lacking in self-confidence, to a fairly determined young man. I knew by then that I wanted to excel, and I'd learned, especially during that final month of the track season, the value of hard work. I wanted to be someone special, and I even had a sense of the direction I was going to take. My high school yearbook said that my ambition was to play professional football.

But, first, I had another dream to fulfill. I was going to college. The only question was which one. I'm kind of sorry that it wasn't M.I.T. Maybe I could have been their first professional lineman.

5

A Rah-Rah Sorority Man

I'LL END THE suspense quick. I'll answer the big question right away. Yes, I did almost get myself killed in college. And I didn't waste any time about it. I'd only been at the University of Idaho for about six weeks. I'd already made some good friends—Jerry Smythe and Larry Norby, who were my classmates, and Pete Shawver, who was a sophomore, and a wonderful girl named Nancy Burns.

I'd been working in the sun all summer, and I'd gotten a deep tan. The sun had bleached my hair almost blond, and I walked around campus all the time in one of those muscle shirts with no sleeves. I really thought I had everything. I must've been the oddest sight you ever saw.

Nancy liked to needle me about how strong and how muscular I thought I was. She was just a friend, a good friend, not a girl friend, and one day she said, "You really think you can do anything, don't you?"

I said something clever, like, "Yup."

"Well, I'll bet you can't ring the SAE bell," she said.

Sigma Alpha Epsilon, one of the fraternities, had a big bell on a balcony on the top floor of its house. The bell was rung only on special traditional occasions, like initiation time or when a virgin walked across the lawn or something like that.

"I'll bet you I can ring the bell," I said. "I'll get Norby and Smythe, and we'll do it."

"I'll bet you a steak dinner," Nancy said.

I couldn't wait to tell Smythe and Norby about our project. It'd be no sweat at all. After all, weren't we freshman football players and pledges to Sigma Nu fraternity, and what could be any better than that? We thought we were really something. "Well, let's get after it," they said.

The University was building a new dormitory, so we went over to the construction site to steal a rope. We needed the rope for the getaway we planned. We figured we'd tie the rope to the railing around the SAE balcony and then slide down the rope to escape. We were lucky. We found a two-inch-thick chunk of Manila, a huge rope, with a big iron hook on the end of it. The rope must've been a hundred feet long and it must've weighed a hundred pounds.

We added Big Pete Shawver to our party, and about two o'clock in the morning, we pulled up in front of the SAE house in my secondhand Studebaker convertible. Smythe waited in the car, the motor running. Big Pete stood outside the house, below the balcony. Norby and I went in the front door and tiptoed up to the second floor. We couldn't go up to the third floor, the top floor, because there was a dormitory up there. Norby and I climbed out a second-floor window to a little ledge, and Norby boosted me up to the overhanging roof. Then he handed me the hundred-pound, hundred-foot rope. The balcony was at the far end of the house, so I crawled up to the peak of the sloping roof, gently made my way the length of the house, then lowered myself onto the balcony. I tied one end of the rope to a corner post of the railing around the balcony, leaving over six feet of rope and the iron hook. Then I slowly lowered the other end of the rope to the ground. Norby, who'd gone back down the stairs, and Big Pete held their end of the rope away from the house, so I could slide down without banging against the walls.

With everything ready, I picked up the iron hook and began ringing the hell out of the bell. It was almost 2:30 by then, and I pounded hard enough to wake up the whole campus. Of course, I woke up the SAEs, too. The balcony was right off their dormitory. As they came running to the balcony, I played Errol Flynn and nimbly, considering that I weighed 220 pounds, leaped over the side of the railing. I had one end of the rope in my hands, and Norby and Pete had the other end in their hands, and the combination was just too much. The railing collapsed. The corner post flew off. I was suddenly in midair, ready to fall three floors. Blindly, without even thinking, I dropped the rope, stuck out my left hand and caught hold of a little rain trough.

I still don't know what the hell a tin rain trough was doing around the base of a balcony, but I clung to it for dear life. Two or three of the SAEs reached down and grabbed me and pulled me back up. I was shaking. They asked me if I wanted a cigarette. I told them that I didn't smoke, but that I'd appreciate a glass of milk. They brought me back into their dorm, gave me a glass of milk, and tried to decide what to do with me. They felt they had to punish me for ringing their bell. "Let's get a toothbrush," somebody said, "and make him scrub the toilets."

They didn't bother with the toothbrush, but they did make me scrub their toilets and their front room and their kitchen. After I'd been working for about an hour, the front door burst open, and Smythe, Norby, and Big Pete charged in, ready to rescue me. They said they'd fight everybody in the house. "Forget it," I told them. "I got caught. Everything's all right. I'll just stay here and scrub the floors. That's fair."

My friends left, and I must've scrubbed for three straight hours. About six in the morning, I looked up and noticed there were only five guys guarding me. I asked one of them to get me a clean bucket of water, and I asked another to get me a glass of milk. I started looking around, and one of the SAEs yelled, "Better get back in here. He's gonna go." I went. I vaulted over a couch and jumped out a window, fell about ten feet to the ground, and hit running. I got back to the Sigma Nu house about 6:30, beat but alive.

Nancy bought me my steak dinner, but it was an expensive free meal. Norby, Smythe, Big Pete, and I had to come up with $17.50 each to pay for the broken railing.

I guess I should have been grateful I was still alive. Once in a while, I stop and wonder why I've always been so accident prone, why I've made such a habit of coming close to death. It's hard to figure out. I'm sure some people'd say that I'm just foolhardy, that I take great risks, but my two major disasters, the incident with the shotgun and the one with the calf, had nothing to do with risks. I wasn't taking any abnormal chances either time. Maybe I'm a little bit careless. I do know this. As far as I can tell, I don't have any physical fears. I'll dive deep down into the Gulf or I'll take over the controls of a plane, without any training in either area, and I won't be frightened at all. And I know, too, that I must have a high threshold of pain; doctors always tell me that. I suppose the lack of fear plus the high threshold of pain lead me into situations that most people would avoid.

I'm not claiming any special bravery. I think the borderline between guts and stupidity is very thin, and I imagine I've stepped on both sides of the line a few times. That's practically the definition of being a professional football lineman.

Sometimes I suspect that the only thing I possess less of than fear is self-discipline. I'm exaggerating. I don't really mean that, because I know I've exercised a great deal of self-discipline in developing myself as a football player and as a businessman. Self-discipline, along with self-knowledge, is absolutely essential in both areas, and I've always pushed myself and pushed myself and pushed myself to succeed. But I often lack self-discipline on a different level.

I have great difficulty at times saying no—no to myself and no to other people. I have trouble depriving myself of good times; I hate to say no to fun. I like people and, as strange as it might sound coming from a big dummy lineman, I don't like to hurt people; I hate to say no to their requests. Maybe that's why, in the five or six months before I entered college, three separate schools—the University of Idaho, Washington State College, and the University of Washington—each thought I was coming to its campus.

Several colleges had been hot after me during the last half of my senior year in high school. Naturally, some of the colleges just looked at my athletic record —all-league tackle in football, the state record in the shot-put. But my marks were respectable, too; I was in the upper fifth of my class. I'd taken a battery of intelligence tests, and I ranked in the top 10 per cent nationally in the natural sciences, the top 25 per cent nationally in reading comprehension. (I hate to admit this, particularly in the middle of my second book, but I ranked in the bottom 20 per cent nationally in mechanics of expression; my grammar was godawful.) I probably looked like a good catch for almost any

school. Idaho's rather isolated, geographically, and
Sandpoint, tucked up in the northern tip, is even
more isolated, so it's not surprising that I didn't at-
tract any nationwide attention. Colleges in the East
and the Southeast and the Midwest and the South-
west ignored me completely. But on the West Coast,
a number of schools showed an interest in me, and I
quickly narrowed down the field to Idaho, Washington, and Washington State.

One of the attractions of Washington State was
Jack Mooberry, its track coach, the fellow who'd taught
me the Parry O'Brien method of putting the shot.
Somehow, I guess, I must've given him the idea I
wanted to go to Washington State because, in May of
my senior year, I got a letter from Dan Stavely, the
freshman football coach. "Looking forward to seeing
you down here next weekend for our state track meet,"
Stavely wrote, "and I hope that you throw the iron
ball a long ways this weekend. Mr. Mooberry asked
me to give you his very best regards and to thank you
for your having thought of him. We are all counting
on having you with us this fall, Jerry, and I am sure
that you will enjoy very much your track and football
competition."

I kept receiving letters from Stavely right up
through August, filled with instructions on how to prepare for freshman football:

"After executing the five exercises given you in
last week's letter, where from a lineman's stance you
spring out lunging with your hands in front, get to
hands and toes, crawl 10 yds., then up to feet for 10
yds. This makes a 20-yd. maneuver. [Obviously,
Stavely didn't think he was getting many math
majors.] This teaches quickness which is a lineman's
bread and butter. . . ."

In May 1954, I visited the University of Washington
campus and met the football coach, John Cherberg,
who later became lieutenant-governor of the state.

"It was a real pleasure to meet and visit with you last weekend," Cherberg wrote me. "I certainly hope that you enjoyed the trip as we were all greatly impressed with you. My purpose in writing is to indicate in a definite way that should you decide to enter the University of Washington, you will be placed upon an athletic job upon which you may earn $75.00 a month. In addition, you will be allowed to apply for Grant-in-Aid for tuition.

"This, of course, is guaranteed by the Athletic Department of the University of Washington for four years or until you complete your eligibility. In the event of injury which would preclude your continuing football, this guarantee would still hold. In return, we should like you to remain the splendid young citizen you are, keep eligible and play football with the desire you have exhibited in the past. . . .

"Will you please let me know your impressions of our splendid school? Perhaps if you could find it possible to visit us again, I would be very happy to personally show you our campus and explain more fully the advantages, scholastically and athletically, of attending the University of Washington."

About six weeks later, Cherberg wrote to me again. "I was happy to learn you are interested in attending the University of Washington," he said. "We are anxious to have a young man of your scholastic and athletic ability attend the University.

"If you would like to come to Seattle and work for the rest of the summer, Mr. Parker Buck of the Eyres Transfer Company has a job for you upon which you can earn approximately $75 a week. . . . The job Mr. Buck has for you is a good, clean one. . . .

"Your personal welfare is our chief interest and we will do everything possible to make your life at Washington interesting, happy and successful."

Even if he was still a football coach, John Cherberg was already a pretty good politician. I'm amused

now, looking back, to see how carefully every mention of athletics was balanced with a mention of
scholastics. I'm sure Cherberg meant it too. He wanted
my strong body and my strong head.

Just about the same time Cherberg was courting
me, the head football coach at the University of Idaho,
Skip Stahley, wrote me and said, "The entire coaching
staff is most pleased to know that you are planning
to become a member of our student body. We are
counting on you heavily as being one of the leaders
on the finest Freshman football team ever assembled
to represent the University of Idaho."

Everyone was counting on me, waiting for me, trying to help me, and I was getting totally confused. I
think I wanted to go to all three schools at once, to
study engineering at the University of Idaho, which
was close to home, and play football at the University
of Washington, which had a big-time schedule and a
big reputation, and put the shot at Washington
State College. I led them all a merry chase, but in my
mind, even though I didn't bother to tell Washington
State, I cut the choice down to Washington or Idaho.

Kenny Armstrong, my high school classmate whose
mother had been my nurse after the shotgun accident, decided definitely that he was going to Washington. (George Kom and Roger Olson, my other buddies,
picked Idaho State, but I wasn't interested in going
there.) During the summer, the University of Washington got Kenny a job in Seattle and offered me a
similar job. I just happened to mention the offer to a
man from the University of Idaho. The same night,
an Idaho representative came to my home and told
me he had a job for me in Moscow, the site of the
University. I drove down to Moscow and, of course,
told the people there that I sure did want to go to
Idaho. They put me in a plane, flew me to Boise,
gave me a job in a sawmill and a room in a boarding
house and hid me, absolutely hid me.

The University of Washington people flew Kenny Armstrong to Boise two or three times in a private plane, searching for me, but Kenny couldn't find me. It didn't make much difference. I'd made up my mind that I wanted to go to the University of Idaho, and the main reason was Skip Stahley.

Back in high school, when I'd been snubbed at our football banquet by that Idaho coach, I'd sworn that I'd never go to Idaho. Even when that coach left, I told myself it still wouldn't affect my feelings; I wouldn't go to Idaho under any circumstances. Then I met Skip Stahley. I met him at a track meet in Boise, the state championships, and he introduced me to Wayne Walker, who was a high school senior in Boise, and said he looked forward to having both of us at Idaho. I didn't know who Wayne was and I didn't much care, but I liked Skip right away. He was just starting his first year at the University, and he was a beautiful man. He was warm and he seemed to have a real interest in me and he thought I was a hell of a football player, much better than I thought I was. The year before, he'd been the backfield coach for the Chicago Cardinals in the National Football League, which had some influence on me, because I was already thinking, vaguely, about pro football. Skip had been coaching for twenty-five years, as an assistant at Harvard and the University of Washington and as head coach at Delaware, Brown, George Washington, and Toledo. He was about my father's age, and he was a fatherly type, and I just liked everything about him. He took me to a football rally during the summer and introduced me to the crowd as a new Idaho Vandal.

John Cherberg didn't give up. He wrote me another letter. "Ken has told me that you had decided to come to [Washington] University and were quite disappointed when local pressure was put on you to remain in Idaho," Cherberg wrote. "The purpose of this little note is to point out, Jerry, that whatever favors they have done for you are now being used as something of a sandbag to influence your decision. May I point out that we at no time have attempted to place you under any obligation whatsoever, but have wanted you to come to your decision of your own free will.

"I am sure that Ken will give you a little better insight on our situation as a result of his experiences. As I wrote you sometime ago, it certainly would not do you any harm to visit our campus, work around the pavilion and find out for yourself what kind of people we are and what kind of a school we have. If you decide not to stay, we will be the first to wish you good luck and God speed. I hope you see the wisdom of this course of action.

"I have already explained the many advantages of attending the University and I am sure Ken will be able to point out more to you. We have a very interesting football practice game scheduled for this Saturday and I should like very much to invite you over to attend this game. I certainly hope you decide to come.

"Please accept my kindest regards and every good wish for your future."

I was tempted to accept the invitation, but I decided against it. My father was happy that I'd chosen Idaho—he'd begun to take an interest in my athletic career, and he said he wanted me close by so that he could watch me play—and he told me not to talk to anyone else from the University of Washington.

I finished my job in Boise and drove home at the end of the summer to pack up for college. Kenny Armstrong flew in from Seattle. "It's all settled," Kenny said. "You're going to Idaho, and I'm going to Washington. We won't see each other much. Let's go over to Spokane tonight, see a movie and celebrate." We drove sixty miles to Spokane and we stopped off to visit some prominent University of Washington alumnus and the next thing I knew, despite my father's advice and my own better judgment, I was flying to Seattle to watch a practice session. I was John Cherberg's guest, and he made me feel like a real big shot.

The Washington people gave a hard sell—they really tempted me with an offer of a one-week salmon-fishing trip—and I listened to them, then slipped out of Seattle and hurried home to Sandpoint. I told my father that Washington promised me a summer job in Alaska and promised to fly him and Mom to every home game. He told me to forget about the University of Washington. He said he didn't want to go flying around to watch me play. That ended the whole discussion, and I wasn't upset at all. I was just happy that I was going to college. My father was more emotional than I'd ever seen him; he gave me a big hug and a kiss when I left for school.

I went off to Moscow, and, at the beginning, I was really a rube. I called up home and told my mother, "I'm going to join one of them sororities." I didn't know the difference between a sorority and a fraternity. I did find out the difference pretty quickly. I'm a very observant fellow.

The first week or two at Idaho, I was kind of unhappy. I'd been promised an athletic job, and it hadn't come through yet, and I felt that I was being cheated. I put in a phone call to Kenny Armstrong in Seattle. "These guys are putting it to me," I said. "I'm not happy."

Kenny called one of the Washington coaches, who called me and said, "Get in your car and leave. We'll transfer you. We'll have somebody get your clothes. We'll do everything. Just get in your car right now and leave."

I'd just pledged Sigma Nu, and I made my call from the fraternity. Less than ten minutes after I got off the phone, Skip Stahley was at the Sigma Nu house. "What's going on?" Skip said. I told him my beefs, and he got it all straightened out, and I decided to stay at Idaho.

For a long time, I wondered about Skip's timing—arriving at the fraternity house just at the critical moment—and finally he told me what had happened. Right from the beginning, he was worried about Washington pursuing me, so he had told one of my fraternity brothers to keep an eye on me and let him know whenever I made or received a long-distance call. Skip believed in thorough planning; I've always had a lot of respect for him.

I've got much less respect for one of the engineering profs at Idaho. I don't remember his name or anything about him, except the stupid thing he did to me. He was teaching one of my first classes, and he said, "Are any of you people in here football players?"

I raised my big, strong, sleeveless right arm, showing off my scars.

"It should either be football or engineering," the professor said.

"I'm in college on a football scholarship," I said.

"Then I recommend that you get out of engineering," he said.

He was an ass, a complete ass. He should've showed me some way I could have stayed in engineering. He should've recommended I switch to a five-year course or even a six-year course, so that I could've spaced out my labs and my tough subjects. Instead, he flatly told me to get out of engineering. I wasn't smart enough to argue with him; I just did what he said. He could've ruined my life. If I'd been seriously injured, I might not have been able to play football any more. I might have been able to finish my college studies, but not in the field I originally wanted. I wouldn't have been prepared in the profession that really interested me. I was lucky, I guess, that I became successful in professional football, but I still wish I'd been able to stay in engineering. If nothing else, I'm sure it would've helped me with the diving company.

But I listened to that dumb professor and dropped out of engineering. For a while, I didn't know what course to study. I didn't want to go into physical education; I figured that was just for the dummies. I finally settled on business administration, but I was lazy and halfhearted about it. It wasn't difficult, and I didn't study, and I got into bad habits. I cut a lot of classes, especially when I found the subject easy. When I got in trouble in a course, then I'd go to class and get my grades up. Temporarily, I sort of stopped being curious, stopped being a learner. I didn't read as much as I had in high school; in fact, I didn't start reading again till I'd been out of college four or five years. At Idaho, much more than in high school, I felt that I was separated from the rest of the student body, that I was a football player first and an individual second.

I goofed around a lot, participating in crazy fraternity stunts, fights and beer baths and all kinds of hellraising. We had some wild crew—Norby and Smythe and Wayne Walker and me. We'd steal the front door off the Beta Theta Pi fraternity house, and we'd throw sacks of manure on their porch. Once the girls from Kappa Kappa Gamma sorority brought a calf's head over to our fraternity house and left it on a table, a cigarette dangling out of its mouth, with a note: "Sigma Nu, we've lost our head over you." That was our idea of really fantastic humor.

Idaho wasn't a very big school—it had maybe three thousand students—and it wasn't very glamorous, and the social life, as far as I was concerned, consisted mostly of movies and parking. I wasn't much of a drinker, especially during the football season, and I was even less of a dancer; on the dance floor, I was good for blocking and tackling and not much else. I never had too much money to spend on socializing, although after a while I began receiving $25 a month from an Idaho alumnus. I think he was paying me for sending him the correct score of the football game each week. Of course, Norby and Smythe found out about my little check, and they watched my mailbox each day and saw to it that we celebrated properly whenever the money arrived.

I started dating Barbara Joseph my first week of school—we met at an orientation class—and we went out for two years and then we got married just before our junior year. Barbara came from a ranch in Oregon, just across the Snake River from Weiser, Idaho. She didn't know much about football and didn't care much, and maybe that's why we got along so well. She was one of the few people at Idaho who didn't look at me as mainly a football player. She looked at me as a person.

Clowning and socializing and sports seemed to be most of my life at Idaho. I enjoyed playing football there, and I certainly stayed in perfect condition. As far as I can remember, I didn't miss one practice in four years, and I know I didn't miss a game. My junior and senior years, playing offensive right guard and defensive middle guard and handling all the place-kicking, I played sixty minutes several games and averaged close to fifty-eight minutes a game. It wasn't that I was so great; we just didn't have too many bodies. I might have made All-American at Washington, but I wouldn't have gotten to play so much football.

When I arrived at Idaho, the school had seen only two winning football seasons in thirty years and not a single winning season since 1938. My class helped keep the record pure. We didn't have a single winning season either, but in our last two years, we came on very strong. We gave some awfully tough teams a hard time.

In my sophomore year, my first varsity season, I was perfect, in a small way, but we were dreadful. I kicked thirteen extra points in thirteen attempts, but we still lost seven games out of nine. My college football career almost ended prematurely. We played a game in San Jose, California, and a teammate named John Russo and I went out to see the sights and got a little carried away and came back to our hotel fifteen minutes late for bed check. Between us, we made up an elaborate story about going to a movie across town and losing track of the time and not being able to get a cab and running all the way back, but we never got a chance to tell the story. When we reached the hotel, an assistant coach was waiting in the lobby. "Skip's waiting for you," he said.

We walked in, and coach Stahley looked at us and said, "You're through. Both of you. Get out of here. You're off the team. Find your own way home."

We didn't know what the hell to do. We didn't even know if we were allowed to go to bed. We went to our rooms, and I don't think either of us slept all night. The next morning, Skip called the team captains into his room and said, "I'm going to leave it up to you boys. You decide what to do with Kramer and Russo. But I think they ought to be punished in some way."

The captains decided that they needed us for the game, that we shouldn't be kicked off the team, but that we should lose a month's tuition from our scholarships. That was about $100, which was an awful lot of money to me at the time; fifty cents was a lot to me. As it turned out, we never lost the money. Skip kept saying each game that if we played well, he'd think about rescinding the fine. He got a lot of good football out of us before he finally told us he'd rescinded the fine.

In my junior season, we lost our first four games, including the opener against Washington 53–21.

Then we suddenly came together as a team and won four of our last five games. Our only late-season loss was to Oregon State, the team that went on to represent the Pacific Coast in the Rose Bowl. Oregon State had won five straight coming into our game; they'd beaten Washington without much difficulty. We got way up for them. I kicked a thirty-five-yard field goal early in the fourth period that put us in front, 10–7. But they scored with five minutes to go and beat us, 14–10. My buddy, Larry Norby, gained 103 yards rushing, only 24 less than the whole Oregon State team. We earned more glory in defeat than we did in our four victories over Utah, Utah State, Fresno State, and Montana, none of which was exactly a powerhouse.

I also competed in track and field at Idaho, and it's all because of putting the shot that I've got my long scar, my zipper, down the back of my neck. During my sophomore year, I competed in a Pacific Coast Conference track meet in California, and when I got back to Moscow, I wasn't prepared for my Monday classes. I decided I'd skip school, but I needed an excuse from a doctor.

Monday morning, I went to the school infirmary and told the doctor that my neck was hurting. Actually, my neck hadn't bothered me at all. The doctor X-rayed me, and said, "Yup, you got a chip in it. I better send you over to an orthopedic man in Spokane."

I went up to Spokane, about ninety miles away, and the orthopedic man looked me over, took his own X rays and said, "Well, it's not doing any harm, but it might someday. It'd probably be a good idea to have that chipped vertebra taken care of right now. The school'll pay for it, and I'll have you up real quick."

"What kind of an incision will it be?" I asked.

Before the goodbyes,
Jerry Kramer
does some reminiscing . . .

The 1962 championship game against the New York Giants was played in New York, but it was real Green Bay weather, miserably cold, the temperature in the teens, the playing field

hard as concrete, and the wind blowing about thirty-five miles an hour. Yankee Stadium scared the hell out of me, anyway. Jim Ringo (51) has just been introduced, and I'm about to leave Coach Lombardi in the dugout and run out onto the field.

Jimmy Taylor blasting through a small hole in the Kansas City line in the first Super Bowl.

1967, Atlanta Falcons. "No more 280-pound tackles to break my ribs."

1967, Detroit Lions. "I'm never going to hit Alex Karras again. I'm never going to be hit by Alex Karras again."

The 1967 Western Division playoff game in Milwaukee against the Los Angeles Rams was one of our biggest wins—a game that started off badly and could have become a disaster when

one of Bart Starr's passes was intercepted and returned to our 10-yard line. But, as always, our defense rose to the occasion and held the Rams off, and soon Bart was controlling the game.

1967, leading Elijah Pitts in the rain against Detroit.

In 1967, on a sunny day against the Falcons, before
I lost a step or two, I pulled out to lead our sweeps.

Travis Williams (23) had a great day against
the Rams in the 1967 playoff.

After our victory in the last fifteen seconds against Dallas for our third straight NFL championship, we all suspected we would be playing our last game for Vince Lombardi in the Super Bowl in Miami against Oakland. Here, I'm leading Donny Anderson off on a long gain.

"The worst part,
I think, is giving
up the way of
life. It is a beautiful
way of life, sharing
setbacks and triumphs
with a group of
guys whose interests,
if not the same
as your own, are at
least similar."

"I doubt that I'll ever be so close again to a group of people
I was to my teammates on the Green Bay Packers. We laughe
together. We swore together. We struggled together. Sure, w
laughed at stupid things sometimes, and we swore unnece
sarily, and we struggled to play a silly game. We were big ki
in many ways. But, damn, it was fun."

"Oh, just a hairline scar," the surgeon said. "Maybe an inch long, at the most. You'll never notice it."

"OK," I said. I figured another tiny little scar wasn't going to destroy my good looks.

The surgeon put me out and took me into the operating room, and when I woke up, I was lying in a hospital bed, my head propped up on a bunch of pillows. The doctor came in to see me, shaking his head. "Well," he said, "I couldn't find it. Couldn't find that chip. I looked and I looked in there, and I couldn't find it." He didn't seem too happy.

"When can I go home?" I said.

"How do you feel?" he said.

My head was killing me. "Fine," I said.

"Well, you can go home this afternoon," he said.

I was in agony. I had no more business leaving that hospital than I had being in it in the first place.

I called Barbara at the University and I said, "Come and get me. Bring a bunch of pillows for the car, and get me out of here."

She drove up and picked me up and took me to Sandpoint so that I could rest for a few days. I know that doctor shouldn't have let me out of the hospital. I believe to this day that he just went into my neck and started cutting and digging and cutting and finally gave up and closed me up with a scar about six inches long. I'm sure he wanted to get me out of that hospital as fast as he could so that nobody else would see what he'd done. Not too long ago, I called the hospital in Spokane to see if I could find out any details about the operation, and a woman in the office said she had no record at all of my being a patient in 1956.

With my beautiful new zipper, I was co-captain of the track team in my junior year, and I set a University of Idaho record by putting the 16-pound shot 52 feet, 6 inches. (In high school, we'd thrown the 12-

pound shot.) Coach Stahley didn't like the idea of me missing spring football, so he came up with a surprise maneuver. For the first time, he decided to have the football team elect its captain at the start of spring practice; he had a feeling I'd be elected. I was elected co-captain, and after the voting, Skip came to me and said, "Well, Jerry, you don't have to participate in spring practice. Of course, you are the co-captain of the team. You just do what you think is right."

What could I do? I played spring football, and I competed in track and field. I had a lovely schedule. At 2 P.M. most days, I'd collect all my football gear— shoulder pads, helmet, kicking shoes, regular shoes —pick up my shot and my discus and carry everything to the athletic field. I'd throw the shot for an hour, then throw the discus for half an hour, then climb over a fence, slip my football equipment over my track shorts and practice place-kicking for half an hour. Then I'd practice with the rest of the football team from 4 o'clock to 6. I got worn out. I finally got to the point where I stopped practicing the shot and the discus and just competed in meets.

The big test of my durability came late in May. The regional meet to qualify for the Pacific Coast Conference track championships and the traditional spring football game were scheduled for the same morning. I went to coach Stahley and said, "Skip, I can't make the football game. I've got a track meet."

"Where at?" he asked.

"Washington State," I said. Washington State's in Pullman, only nine or ten miles from Moscow.

"What time's your event?"

"I don't know."

"Find out."

I found out my event was going to start at 10:30 and I told coach Stahley, and he announced that the spring football game would begin at 1 P.M. So I competed in the track meet in the morning and qualified for the Pacific Coast championships, then rushed back to Moscow and played most of the spring football game. I think I was about ready to die.

In my senior year of football, we opened our season against Oregon, the team that went to the Rose Bowl that year. We held them pretty well, but they beat us 9–6. We won only one and tied one of our next four games, but then, with another late-season rush, we won three in a row and came to the final game of the year, against Washington State, with a record of four victories, three defeats, and a tie. We had a chance to become the first Idaho team in twenty years to finish above .500.

We didn't make it. We were losing by only one point, 14–13, when, on the final play of the third quarter, I twisted my knee. It wasn't anything serious, but I missed the whole last quarter, and Washington State beat us 21–13. Still, I was pretty happy with the year. I made second-team All-Pacific Coast Conference at guard and made a few All-American honorable mentions, but, just as in high school, I didn't get too much attention outside my own area. I was just a pretty good ballplayer on a team with an unexciting record, and I never met a single scout from the National Football League. I did get telegrams from San Francisco and Pittsburgh and maybe a couple of others, and letters from half a dozen clubs, including one from the Green Bay Packers that was real personal. It began something like, "Dear Football Player . . ." Everbody wanted to know my vital statistics, height, weight, speed, stuff like that, and whether I was interested in playing pro football. Of course I was.

On the day of the pro football draft, I heard that I'd been picked by Green Bay in the fourth round, which was pretty good for an unknown lineman, a lot higher than I'd expected. I ran into an English class to tell Wayne Walker, and a few hours later, we found out that he'd been drafted in the fourth round, too, by Detroit.

Wayne and I went out and celebrated. The next thing I did was try to find out where Green Bay was.

The Packers had a scout living in Lewiston, thirty-five or forty miles away, and he came to see me with maps and clippings about Green Bay and its team. Green Bay looked to me like a nice little resort town; I thought I might feel at home. Then I checked the Packers' record. They'd just finished ten years without a winning season; I knew I'd feel at home.

I had to think a little about whether I wanted to turn pro right away at the end of the football season. If I did, I wouldn't be eligible for track and field. Both the Packers and the Vancouver Lions in Canada wanted to sign me, and I also had an offer to play, for pay, in the annual Senior Bowl game in Mobile, Alabama.

Barbara and I had had our first child, Tony, just before the start of our senior year. I didn't have much money saved up from my summer jobs—her parents had been helping us out—so I decided I had to turn pro. When I went down to San Francisco to play, for charity, in the East-West game, I talked to Lisle Blackbourn, then the Packer coach. My coach, Skip Stahley, had told me that he figured if I could get $7,000 for my first year, I'd be doing pretty good. I told Blackbourn I wanted $8,000, plus a bonus for signing. I guess I hadn't entirely wasted my business administration schooling. Blackbourn offered me $7,500, and we argued, and, finally, he agreed to give me a $250 bonus for signing and a contract for $7,750, which depended, of course, on me making the team.

After I played in the East-West game, I signed with Green Bay, then went down to the Senior Bowl. I kind of regretted giving up my track eligibility. I still feel that if I'd really concentrated on the shot-put that spring, if I'd put the same effort into it that I'd put into track and football combined the previous year, I could have gotten up around fifty-seven or fifty-eight feet, which would have been tremendous at that time. But I never got a chance. I dropped out of track and field.

I also dropped out of school that spring. I felt that I owed it to my wife and my young son to get out and earn a living. I'd been working part time in a foundry, murderous, hot, physical work, and I went to work full time. I never got my college degree, a fact that still bothers and embarrasses me. It was plain stupid of me to give up the degree when I was so close. I could have been in real trouble if professional football hadn't worked out. Now that I've got enough perspective to look back objectively, I realize it's not only the degree I miss. I know now that a college degree doesn't necessarily make a man bright. What frustrates me now, more than anything else, is the way I wasted my time academically in college. There's so much I want to know now, so much I could have learned back in college if I'd given up a few beers and a few parties. Partly, I still blame that professor who talked me out of engineering, but mostly I blame myself. It was my own fault that, when I walked out of the University of Idaho, I was really prepared to do only one thing. I had no choice. I had to succeed at professional football.

6

Think "Win"

DURING MY FOUR years at the University of Idaho, the four years since my Sandpoint High team had come within one game of a perfect season, I had forgotten what victory, consistent victory, was like. I knew how it felt to win one game at a time, but I'd stopped thinking like a winner. At Idaho, our best perform-ances, it seemed, were always in defeat, to Oregon State, to Oregon, to Washington State. We learned to be happy with "almost."

The Green Bay Packers shared the same defeatist attitude. They hadn't even come close to winning a division title since the end of World War II. Their players didn't know the meaning of pressure because they'd never participated in a crucial game. To them, the major importance of each game was that it was one less to play.

In 1958, my first professional season, I, like all the Green Bay Packers, played and accepted the role of a loser. But in 1959 and 1960, I took a refresher course in victory. I started, with the rest of the team, at the bottom and, under expert tutelage, rode to the top. My professor was Vincent Thomas Lombardi, and in a season, probably in a week, he taught me more about the basic ingredients of success, in life as well as in football, than I had learned in four rather misused years of higher education.

Early in 1958, I received my huge $250 bonus from the Green Bay Packers. I also received $500 for playing in the Senior Bowl. In March, I traded in a three-year-old Chevy and purchased my first new car, a Chevrolet Impala convertible. The trade-in covered the down payment, and I arranged for the monthly installments to begin in September. By then, I figured, I'd be drawing a regular salary from professional football. If I hadn't made it in the National Football League, I guess I would have had to give up my car.

In July, I left my wife and year-old son in Idaho and reported to the College All-Star training camp outside Chicago. I weighed 235 pounds, ten pounds above my college playing weight, and when I reached camp, I found myself surrounded by guys I'd read about in the papers, famous All-Americans like John David Crow and King Hill and Lou Michaels and a funny-looking guy named Alex Karras. Wayne Walker was the one familiar face, and I got to know a few future Packers, Dan Currie and Jimmy Taylor and Ray Nitschke. There were a bunch of good guards in camp, including Bill Krisher of Oklahoma and Joe Niceli of West Virginia and Tony Stremic of Navy, and at first I thought I was just lucky to be in such company. It took a few days before I suspected I might be as good as anyone else.

The other linemen kidded Currie and me about going to a weak club like Green Bay. Currie was friendly with Karras and Michaels—the All-America set —and they teased us all the time. Dan himself wasn't too happy about going to Green Bay; he'd been All-American at Michigan State, and he'd dreamed of playing at home, for the Detroit Lions, the NFL champions. But Green Bay had made him its number-one draft selection, so Dan had no choice.

I began to have mixed feelings about Green Bay. John Sandusky, who coached the linemen in the College All-Star game, had played with Green Bay in 1956. John took me aside after a week or so of training and said, "You'll play in the NFL, but not with Green Bay. You won't make that club. They've got five veteran guards returning."

I couldn't argue with Sandusky. He knew more about the NFL in general, and the Packers in particular, than I did. Besides, I wasn't even sure I was playing the proper position. "Your best shot at the pros," Skip Stahley, my Idaho coach, had told me, "is at middle guard. Your second best shot is at defensive end, and your third best is at offensive guard." Most of the pro teams had stopped using a middle guard, the man opposite the center on a five-man defensive line; with the increasing emphasis on passing, they'd gone to the four-three defense. I'd played some defensive end in college, and I really loved that spot. But the Packers had told me they were planning to try me as an offensive guard, and the All-Stars were using me as an offensive guard, and I never did get a chance anywhere else. Sometimes, even now, I wonder if Skip Stahley was right; I might've been a hell of a defensive end, might even have forced my roomie, Willie Davis, into retirement a few years early.

Early in the All-Star training camp, Bill Krisher and I were both playing right guard. Krisher had been everybody's All-American, and I beat him out, which surprised me as much as him. But I hurt my knee in our scrimmage against the Chicago Bears and missed a few days of practice, and when I came back, Krisher had the job locked up. Sandusky switched me to left guard, and I beat out Joe Niceli for the starting assignment. I began thinking I must be a pretty good ballplayer.

I'll never forget the All-Star game against Detroit. It had to be the biggest athletic thrill of my life up to that time. We were all nervous as hell. We kept telling ourselves that the Lions weren't supermen, that they put on their pants one leg at a time, same as us, but we didn't really believe it. We were a little awed.

At the start of the game, they introduced the All-Stars one by one. Soldiers' Field in Chicago was dark, and the spotlight hit each man as he trotted through the goal posts to the middle of the field. Dan Currie, our starting center, ran out first. I think he got either the game ball or a kiss from the All-Star queen. Dan was so tense he probably couldn't have told the difference, anyway; he almost tripped going through the goal posts. I ran out second, and I thought for sure that I was going to stumble, that in his first big national appearance, the dummy from Idaho would fall flat on his face. But I made it. I survived. We really took it to the Lions. We were all fired up, and they kind of took us for granted, and we beat them 35–19. It was a perfect lesson in the value of motivation, and it was a wonderful introduction to professional football.

The very next night, I made my first appearance in a Packer uniform. Green Bay played the Pittsburgh Steelers in Milwaukee, and I got thrown in on the kickoff team and the kickoff-return team. We played in a miserable rainstorm, and the Steelers beat us 3–0.

I wasn't too impressed by the Packers. Hell, one night I'd played with a bunch of college guys and we'd whipped the world champions, and the next night I'd played with the Packers, and we'd lost to Pittsburgh. How could I be impressed? Besides, in the back of my mind, I kept thinking about what John Sandusky had said, how I couldn't possibly make the team. As a result, I had a lackadaisical attitude. I didn't worry. I didn't put out 100 per cent. We won the next couple of exhibitions against the Eagles and the Giants, but I didn't do much.

Scooter McLean, who'd succeeded Lisle Blackbourn as coach of the Packers, called me into his office the day after the Giant game and chewed me out. Scooter never yelled much, but he was upset with me. "Jerry," he said, "what in hell's wrong with you? You've got size and speed, but one play you look great and the next play you look like you're out to lunch. What the hell's the matter?"

I told Scooter what Sandusky had said to me. I told Scooter I was just marking time, waiting to be traded.

"We got you to play you, not to trade you," Scooter said.

He meant it. He started me in the next exhibition against Washington, and I happened to get up against a guy who wasn't too fancy, who didn't shake a lot, and I had a good game. I blocked the guy well, drove him well, had no real problems with him.

The next day, McLean cut two of his veteran guards, Al Barry and Joe Skibinski, and both of them were picked up by the New York Giants. Barry, in fact, had a great year with the Giants; he played so well that Vince Lombardi, who was then coaching the New York line, said, "I'd like to see that guard who's as good as Barry."

When I heard about Barry and Skibinski, I immediately called my wife in Idaho and said, "Honey, I think we've got the club made. They cut two veterans." It looked like I was going to be able to pay for my car.

McLean finally decided to keep two veteran guards, Jim Salsbury and Hank Bullough as regulars, plus one rookie guard, either me or Kenny Gray, who later became an All-Pro guard with the St. Louis Cardinals. Kenny had played defensive tackle as well as offensive guard, and he'd looked good at both positions, and he thought he'd be kept. He was the last man cut from the Packer squad. The day they released him, I saw him downtown and waved hello to him, not knowing he'd been cut, and Kenny looked at me and said, "You sonuvabitch, you had a no-cut contract, didn't you?"

At the time, I didn't even know what a no-cut contract was.

"No, I didn't," I said.

"I'll never believe you," he said.

To this day, Kenny probably still thinks I had a no-cut contract.

The atmosphere was really strange in Green Bay that year, particularly strange in light of the atmosphere that followed. It was all kind of gray and vague, without any direction or purpose. For one thing, there was no team unity at all, just a bunch of little cliques. The top group was the McGee-Hornung-Ron Kramer-Howie Ferguson crowd, the real socializers. They played poker for big money, hundreds of dollars changing hands. They had a ball every day. I was just a rookie, just a kid; I stuck pretty much with a couple of other West Coast rookies, Jim Shanley from Oregon and Joe Francis from Oregon State.

Excellence meant absolutely nothing. I remember in our exhibition game against the Giants, somebody threw a long pass to Max McGee and he just stuck a hand up and didn't make any more effort than the man in the moon to catch the ball. He slapped it with his hand and knocked it up in the air and then caught it when it came down. Max made a big gain on the play, but he couldn't have cared less. That was sort of typical of the whole season. If you did something, you did it, and if you didn't, don't worry about it; there were much more important things to do after the game.

Our practice sessions were like picnics. We'd have a little fun and a little kidding around and very little conditioning. We watched the game movies each week, I suppose, but I can't remember a thing about them. There was no great ass-chewing for mistakes, no screaming, no noise, no emphasis on fundamentals or on anything else. There's one good way to measure how undemanding the Green Bay life was in 1958. At the end of the season, I weighed 252 pounds. I'd gained seventeen pounds during a twelve-game season.

Scooter McLean was a great guy, a damn nice guy who seldom got angry and seldom raised his voice. He was just one of the guys. We'd be playing in the little poker game, a quarter or a four-bit limit, and Scooter'd sit down and play with us. I think every man on the club liked him, and I think every man on the club took advantage of him. He actually put us on an honor system for curfew and training rules, and it was like a license to steal. Every guy was able to rationalize his own actions. How could any guy feel that he was hurting this team? The only thing that would have really hurt us was a longer schedule.

The stars of the team were Billy Howton, an end, Bobby Dillon, a defensive halfback, and Jim Ringo; they were our All-Pro candidates. Hornung played fullback most of the year and led us in rushing and in scoring and in everything except hours slept. The quarterbacks were Babe Parilli and Bart Starr, and I swear I have absolutely no recollection of Bart at all. He threw more than 150 passes that year, so I must've seen a lot of him, but he made no impression. He was a complete blank.

I broke into the starting lineup for the first time in our fifth game, against the Philadelphia Eagles. We almost blew a 38–7 lead, but we managed to beat the Eagles 38–35 for our only victory of the year. McLean started me again the following week, against Baltimore. The Colts whipped us 56–0, and the man playing against me, Artie Donovan, whipped me even worse. Artie was one of the great tackles, and I think he taught me more that night than I've ever learned from a tackle since. He jigged and he jogged and he faked and he feinted and he stepped one way and he went the other and he threw a leg out to tease me, and I don't believe I hit him once the whole game.

After one series of plays, I walked back to the bench and I turned to Nick Skorich, our line coach, and I said, "What am I doing wrong? What's happening?"

"Keep your eyes up," Skorich said. "You're ducking your head."

So I kept my eyes up, and I didn't duck my head, and I kept my feet moving, and I couldn't touch Artie Donovan. He was built like a beer barrel, but he had so much agility, so much lateral mobility. He drove me out of my mind—and out of the starting lineup at the end of the first half. When the game was over, I wanted to walk up to Donovan and punch him, just so that I could tell myself he was real, he was substantial, he did have flesh and bones to make contact with.

We went out to the West Coast for our last two games of the year, against San Francisco and Los Angeles, knowing that if we didn't win one or both of those games, Scooter would lose his job. No Packer team in history had ever won less than two games. We really liked Scooter, and we really wanted to win for him, but we didn't know how to win. Instead, we made Packer history. We lost both games, and Scooter didn't wait to be fired. He quit and ran to Detroit as an assistant coach.

During the week between the two West Coast games, a bunch of us went to a restaurant in Los Angeles for dinner and bumped into Curley Lambeau, the man who had started the Packers and had coached them for twenty-nine years, from 1921 through 1949, the golden days of Green Bay football. Curley mentioned to us that he'd heard from some people in Green Bay, asking him to come back and start coaching again, and we all thought that would be a wonderful thing, that would really be terrific.

I went home to Idaho and spent a lot of time thinking about what it was going to be like playing for Curley Lambeau. The man was a legend in Green Bay. Everything I'd heard about him sounded encouraging.

Then I heard the Packers had picked a new coach, and his name wasn't Curley Lambeau. His name was Vince Lombardi. I had one immediate reaction. "Who the hell is Vince Lombardi?" I said.

When I found out that he was an assistant coach for the New York Giants, I thought the Packers had made the dumbest move in the world. They'd hired a guy who'd never been a head coach in his life, who'd never proven himself. How stupid could they be?

I had my first experience with Lombardi on the telephone. Jim Salsbury and Hank Bullough had announced their retirements at the end of the 1958 season, which made me the only returning guard. The Packers sent me a contract for $8,000, and I felt I deserved more. I sent the contract back unsigned, and they sent it back to me. The contract traveled back and forth three times. Finally, I got on the phone with Lombardi. "I'll tell you what," Vince said. "We'll give you $8,300 plus a $1,000 bonus if you get six blocking awards."

"What's a blocking award?" I said.

"The coaches will grade you on your performance in each game," Vince said, "and if you attain a certain percentage, you'll receive a blocking award."

I thought that sounded pretty fair. If I play well, I'll get a bonus, and if I don't play well, I don't deserve it.

I hadn't learned anything about Lombardi yet. During the 1959 season, I earned four blocking awards in the first six games, and earned only one the rest of the year.

The first time I met Vince Lombardi was in July 1959. Joe Francis and I flew in to Green Bay five days earlier than we had to report, even two days before the rookies reported. Joe and I thought we'd play a little golf, have a few laughs, just relax until training camp opened for the veterans. We went to the Packer business office and told Jack Vainisi, who ran the office, that we needed a place to stay. "The dormitory's not open yet," Jack said.

"Well, you've got to get us a motel room or something," we said. "We don't have any money." We had enough money for a good time, but we didn't have any to waste on something like a room.

"Can't do it," Jack said. "I just can't do it."

We argued with him, and Lombardi happened to walk by with a stack of papers in his hand. Jack introduced us to him. "Hi, coach," I said. "Nice meeting you."

"What's the problem?" Vince said.

"Well," I said, "we need a place to stay."

"Put them in the dormitory," Lombardi said to Vainisi. His voice meant do it and do it now. Vainisi had the dorm opened for us, and we moved in, and the next day we played golf and didn't see Lombardi. The following morning, when the rookies were coming in, we bumped into Lombardi on the stairs.

"Where you going?" he said.

"To play golf," I said.

"When you're in the dormitory," said Lombardi, "you make all meals, all practices, all meetings, and all curfews, just like everybody else."

The way Vince said it, there wasn't any question about it, there wasn't any thought of moving into a motel, there wasn't any, "Aw, coach, you know . . ." It was a fact. It was the way it was going to be. Joe

Francis and I knew damn well that we had better make every meeting, every meal, every practice, every curfew. It was a very rude awakening.

The whole arrival of Lombardi was an awakening. "Gentlemen," he told us, right at the beginning, "I have never been associated with a losing team, and I do not intend to start now." Until he came to Green Bay, we had been expected to lose. He was the first person to tell us, without a smile, that we were not going to be losers. We knew immediately that the man was serious, that he actually believed he could make us into a winning team. He made us believers too.

I roomed with Jimmy Taylor in 1959, and the first week of training camp, we discovered how serious Lombardi was about his 11 o'clock curfew. He came into our room one night exactly at 11, and Jimmy was sitting on the side of his bed, in his shorts and socks, and Vince said that the 11 o'clock curfew meant in bed and lights out, and he fined Jimmy $25 for sitting on the side of the bed.

(After a few years with Lombardi, one of our guys figured out a way he could obey the curfew and still enjoy a certain kind of social life. He started getting up at 5 A.M. and meeting his fiancées at 5:30. His technique raised a pretty good philosophical point: When does curfew end and getting up early begin? The question never was settled. His fiancées got tired of the schedule before Lombardi heard about it.)

One night, Dan Currie and Jess Whittenton and Fuzzy Thurston and I decided to sneak out after curfew. We made it away from the dormitory at St. Norbert College in West De Pere, just outside Green Bay, without much difficulty. Then we went to a bar in Green Bay. We were having a good time, drinking a few beers and giggling, and Red Cochran, our backfield coach, walked in. I hid behind the bar. Fuzzy and Jess ran into the john. Dan just kind of crouched down; he didn't know what to do.

Finally, Dan said, "Oh, what the hell, ole Red'll never tell. Ole Red's a good fella." So Dan got up and said hello to Red, and I came out from behind the bar, and Jess and Fuzzy came out of the john, and Red Cochran looked at us and said, "Couldn't you guys have picked another spot? Why the hell did you have to come in here? Why did you have to pick my place?" Red shook his head, looking kind of sad, and said, "I'm going to leave here and I'm going to come back in twenty minutes and I don't want to see any of you here then. If I do, I'm going to have to report you."

Red left, and we thought about leaving, but Dan Currie kept saying, "Old Red'll never tell on us. Good ole Red." When Red Cochran returned, we were still there. Ole Red wasn't very happy to see us. He chased us back to St. Norbert.

The next day, around noontime, between the morning and the afternoon practice sessions, we were resting in the dorm, wondering whether Red had said anything to Lombardi. Then I heard Vince coming down the hall, clickety-clack, clickety-clack, like some storm trooper coming to inspect his prisoners. "THURSTON!" You could've heard Lombardi's roar in Chicago. "THURSTON! What in the hell are we going to do with you? Are you crazy, or what? What in the hell do you think we're running here, a country club? That'll cost you $100."

I could hear Lombardi advancing toward my room. Dan Currie was sitting with me, and we both started looking at our shoes, studying the laces. "KRAMER!" Vince came into the room, blue in his face. "You ought to have your nut checked, mister," he shouted. "That's $100."

The fines weren't nearly so bad as the tongue-lashings Vince gave us. We felt lucky to survive. But Vince wasn't through with us yet. At the end of practice that afternoon, he yelled, "You four guys, come over here. You four guys who broke curfew, come here."

We sprinted over to Lombardi, nervous but obedient. "Start right here on the goal line," he said, "and go down the sideline to the other goal line, then go across the end zone, up the other side of the field and back to here." Vince had pointed out a 300-yard course. "And I want you to play leapfrog all the way."

"What?" said Fuzzy.

"Aw, no," said Dan.

"Get down and start doing them," said Lombardi.

I got down, and Jess got down, and Dan got down, and Fuzzy got down, and we started playing leapfrog. All of us were pretty good at it, except Fuzzy. He was kind of squat and short, not built for leapfrog, and he kept bumping us with his butt or knocking us down, and, about halfway around, we started giggling. Dan was really burned at the whole idea, but even he had to laugh at Fuzzy. It got to the point where, when Fuzzy'd put his hands on our back, we'd sort of duck to make it easier for him to get over. He'd still fall on his head half the time. There must've been two or three thousand people across the street from the field. They'd been watching the practice session, and now they wondered what the hell we were doing. A rumor spread around that the new coach had just invented a new conditioning exercise, and we were just trying it out for him.

Even when we didn't break curfew, Vince worked us like hell. He had us doing grass drills from the start, the tortuous up-downs, not as many as we did in later years, but enough to drive us all to the brink of exhaustion. At the end of each practice, everyone had to run a full lap around the playing field, 300 yards, and the last three guys to finish had to run an extra lap. For each little move in practice that wasn't 110 per cent, Lombardi would order extra laps. "Take a lap, Hornung," he'd scream. "Take a lap, Thurston."

If somebody really goofed up, he'd say, "And take a second lap, take a third lap," and, pretty soon, we began to realize that it was a lot smarter to put out every ounce of energy during practice than to work after practice. He'd stand and holler at you while you took your laps, too. He was harsh and demanding, but he treated everyone equally on the practice field; he played no favorites. Nobody worked any harder than Dave Hanner, a big defensive tackle from Arkansas; Dave seemed to spend alternate days in the hospital, recovering from heat prostration, and on the field, suffering heat prostration.

Several years later, I met a very successful businessman who gave me his definition of the successful person: "He can do, and will do, things that an unsuccessful person can't do, or won't do." Lombardi showed us what we could do, and he made certain that we would do it. He pounded success into us.

From the first day, of course, Lombardi was a master of psychology. He'd beat us and beat us and beat us, till we thought we were no good at all, till we were ready to sink into the ground, and then he'd say something that would send our bodies and our spirits soaring. "Son," he told me one day, after cutting me to ribbons in practice, "one of these days, you're going to be the greatest guard in football." He was absolutely beautiful.

He destroyed the defeatist attitude that had afflicted the Packers for so many years. Fifteen men who had played for Green Bay in 1958 did not play for Green Bay in 1959. The normal turnover is five or six guys, maybe eight at the most, but we lost fifteen men from the team that had won only one game. Some retired, and some Lombardi traded, and some he cut, but one way or another, he got rid of people who had grown comfortable with defeat. He replaced them with people who knew victory, people who could think "win." Vince picked up Em Tunnell, who'd been with the

New York Giants when they were world champions. He picked up Fuzzy Thurston, who'd been with the Baltimore Colts when they were world champions. He picked up Willie Davis and Bill Quinlan and Henry Jordan, who'd played for the Cleveland Browns. Henry got to our training camp three or four weeks after it had opened, and he thought he reported to us in shape; he lost fifteen pounds the first week. These guys were all winners, by experience and by nature. Quinlan had a vicious tongue, and when any of us didn't act like winners, he'd chew us as bad as Lombardi.

Lombardi knew how to handle each individual. He adopted Paul Hornung, told Paul that he was going to be his permanent halfback, that he was going to run and pass and catch passes, the way that Frank Gifford had operated for the Giants. Paul had gotten pretty discouraged with professional football his first two seasons. After coming out of Notre Dame as the golden boy, the Heisman Trophy winner, he'd had a miserable time. Paul always had a star personality, and he loved Vince for telling him he could be a star again. Paul didn't change his ways off the field; he still lived every minute. But he changed his ways on the field; he killed himself every minute, killed himself for Vince.

Somehow or other, in a way I'll never completely understand or be able to explain, Lombardi worked his magic on Bart Starr. No one, absolutely no one, expected Bart to become a great quarterback. His physical equipment wasn't impressive; he wasn't particularly big or particularly strong, and he didn't have an exceptional arm. His background wasn't impressive, either; he was a seventeenth-round draft choice off an Alabama team that didn't win a single game. He might've had tremendous football intelligence even then, but nobody noticed it. And he certainly wasn't a leader; most of the time, we didn't even know Bart was around. He was quiet, almost bashful, but Lombardi saw the spark in him, and nursed the spark. Bart became our starting quarterback late in the 1959 season, and he led us to victories, something he had never done before.

Lombardi did not waste any time shaping us into an efficient machine. It wasn't any gradual thing. Everything he did helped. He was a master of organization; every practice session had a flow, a crispness, that guaranteed maximum benefits. He was a master of detail; he drilled and drilled and drilled to polish our special teams—our kicking and receiving units. He told us repeatedly that one critical play could decide any game and that we'd never know when the critical play was coming up. Even a dummy from Idaho could see that Lombardi had a fantastic football mind; everything the man said made sense. He practically had a fetish about making us come off the ball fast, making us spring into action the split-second the ball was centered. He forced us to practice that a million times, and he made us see how much it meant, how much of an advantage it gave us over the defensive players. He taught us his system of running to daylight; on most plays, we blockers had the option of which way to move our man, and then the runner had the responsibility of finding the hole. When Vince told you to do something, he told you why. He let you know how it would help you individually and how it would help the team, and then you went out and did it.

Lombardi taught us to act first class and think first class. He bought us all green blazers with gold Packer emblems, and he told us to wear our blazers on road trips and to wear them with dress shirts and ties. He wanted us to be proud of being Green Bay Packers.

With his system, he even made me proud to be an offensive lineman. Generally speaking, there's nothing more anonymous than playing guard. After they announce the lineups, you never hear your name over the loudspeaker. You never hear, "Tackle by Kramer," or "Kramer gained eight yards." You're unknown. But in Lombardi's offensive system, with the guards pulling and leading the attack, Fuzzy Thurston and I emerged from obscurity. We still didn't hear anyone announce, "Block by Kramer," or "Block by Thurston," but every time there'd be a photograph in the papers of Hornung scoring a touchdown—which was pretty often over the next few years—there'd be me or Fuzzy or both of us in the picture, leading the way. The same thing was true on television; Paul was the star, and we were only the supporting cast, but we managed to sneak our mugs into almost every scene. That way, we started getting reputations; we were the rarest of beasts, totally visible guards, and it didn't hurt us at all when it came time to pick All-Pro teams.

Four weeks after all of us met Vince Lombardi for the first time, we began our exhibition season. We won four of six exhibitions, which didn't mean too much, but it certainly helped our spirit. I remember in the final exhibition game, against the Washington Redskins, I was beginning to get a little cocky. I was up against Bob Toneff, who'd been an All-Pro defensive tackle, and we were winning so I thought I'd try a little trick on him. It was probably the first time I'd ever experimented as a pro. I got down in my stance, really dug my cleats into the ground as if I were going to pop right into Toneff, and I leaned way forward. He thought sure the play coming up was a run. He submarined. He tried to go under me. I just fell on top of him, and I said, "Hey, Toneff, I was only fooling. It's a pass." He was burned. He didn't care about anything in the game after that except throwing forearms and knees at me. For my physical safety, I decided to keep my funny remarks to myself from then on.

To the amazement of anyone who didn't know Lombardi, we won our first three regular season games. In the opener, we beat the Chicago Bears—we'd lost to them seven of the previous eight times we'd played them—and immediately the whole season was a success. We carried Lombardi off the field after the game. Then we beat the Lions and the 49ers, and you'd have thought God had settled in Green Bay. The whole town went crazy.

I remember I'd lost my shaving kit somewhere, and I went to Holtzer's drugstore downtown to buy a new one. I walked into the store and explained to John Holtzer, the owner, what I needed, and he said, "Here, here's just what you need."

"How much is that?" I said.

"No, no, no," he said. "It's yours. Keep it."

John gave me shaving cream and he gave me a razor, and he happened to see me glance at a pie, and he pushed that on me. It got embarrassing. There were some other things I needed, but I couldn't ask for them, because John wouldn't let me pay for them. The people were just like that all over Green Bay, fantastic.

That's when the love began on the Green Bay Packers, the love that we players felt for each other. Lombardi made us feel that each man on the squad shared in each victory. We were in the clouds. Football was really a pleasure again, the exhilarating experience it hadn't been all during my rookie season. I liked being a winner.

We slumped in the middle of the season. Jimmy Taylor burned his hand in a freak kitchen accident and had to come out of the lineup for several games, and we lost five straight. But we lost to good teams, and we gave the Baltimore Colts—who'd beaten us 56-0 the year before—a terrific struggle before we lost by four points. The Colts went on to win the NFL championship.

Lombardi wouldn't let us think like losers. He kept telling us we'd come back, and we did. We won our last four games, and we finished in third place in the Western Conference. We were the first Green Bay team to enjoy a winning season in twelve years.

Vince, of course, was as happy as he could ever be without finishing first, and the city of Green Bay shared his pleasure. When we got back from our final game, in San Francisco, a huge crowd met us at the airport, and the Minutemen, a local civic group, gave each of us a billfold with a $50 bill in it and a green-and-gold Packer blanket with our name on it.

I spent most of the off-season looking forward to 1960, convinced that we would do even better. Nobody showed up at training camp in 1960 even a little bit out of shape; Lombardi had made physical fitness nuts out of us all.

We won six straight exhibitions, then, after losing our opening game to the Chicago Bears by three points, we won five of our next six. We were tied with the Baltimore Colts for first place in the Western Conference.

Then we played the Los Angeles Rams in Milwaukee. In the third quarter, on a 42-trap play, basically a run through the left guard's spot, I pulled and trapped Lamar Lundy, the Rams' defensive end. I slammed into him and actually hit him either in the knee or the thigh with my head. That's not a joke. He didn't knee me; I headed him. The collision knocked me goofy. I remember seeing stars and staggering back to the huddle and hearing somebody ask me, "Are you all right?"

"I don't know," I said.

I took a time-out and shook my head and went back to the huddle and said, "I'm OK." Bart called a play, and I got up to the line of scrimmage and, suddenly, I realized I didn't know what I was supposed to do on that particular play. I turned to Forrest Gregg, playing tackle next to me, and I whispered, "What do I do?"

"Block that man in front of you," Forrest whispered back.

"OK."

I played that way through the third and fourth quarters. Sometimes I'd turn to Jim Ringo, on the other side of me, and ask him what to do, and he'd say, "Pull, you dummy, it's a forty-nine." I didn't know one play from another.

I had a concussion, which wasn't a totally new experience; I'd had one or two in college, too, and, in a way, they're kind of fun—afterward. It's fun to watch the movies of a game and see yourself doing things that you can't remember ever doing.

It reached the point late in the Rams game where I didn't even bother whispering. "Tell me what to do now," I said to Forrest once.

"Block him," Forrest said, nodding toward the tackle in front of me.

George Strugar, the Los Angeles tackle, looked at us like we were crazy. He didn't think any offensive linemen would be stupid enough to discuss their blocking assignments out loud. But I didn't have any choice; I couldn't make a move on my own. The Rams beat us by two points and knocked us out of first place. After the game, I noticed a small, bright fluorescent spot in front of my eye.

I didn't realize it at the time, but I had suffered more than a concussion. I came out of the Los Angeles game with a detached retina in my left eye. But I figured the only reason the eye was bothering me was because of my concussion, and I tried not to pay any attention to it.

Five days later, on Thanksgiving, we played the Lions in Detroit—Alex and his friends—and I played the whole game and we got beat again. All of a sudden, we were in bad shape.

Our record was 5-4, and the Colts were 6-2, and it looked like we were just about out of the race. But

Baltimore lost its next game, to San Francisco, and we jumped back in contention, one full game behind the Colts, half a game behind the Chicago Bears, who were 5-3-1. San Francisco was tied with us at 5-4, and the Lions, in fifth place, were 4-5. It was a hell of a battle.

We went to Chicago to play the Bears, and this turned out to be one of the most significant games in my whole Packer career, partly because of what it meant in the Western Conference race and partly because, for the first time, Bart Starr showed me and the whole team that there was a lot of steel in him. Bart had begun the season as our second-string quarterback, behind Lamar McHan, and he had moved into the regular lineup after three or four games. He'd played pretty well for us, but there was still some suspicion that he might be a bit of a pussycat, a little delicate, a little fragile, maybe even a little short of guts. In the Bear game, Bart destroyed all the suspicions.

Early in the game, Bill George, the Bears' great linebacker, red-dogged. He shot through the line and got right to Bart and busted him in the mouth, knocked him down, and cut up his lip. The blood started trickling out of Bart's mouth, and George looked at him and said, "I'm going to take care of you, Starr, you pussy."

Bart got up, spitting blood, and unleashed a steady stream of profanity at Bill George, all the choice words, all the really mean ones. I think that was the first, and probably the last, time I ever heard Bart swear, and he came back strong, tough, and unafraid. He established a controlled, intelligent attack.

We led the Bears at half time by only 13-7, but in the second half, Bart completed nine out of ten passes—including his first two touchdown passes of the season—and we beat Chicago 41-13. I began to believe in Bart Starr that day, and I've believed in him ever since.

Baltimore lost to Detroit the same afternoon, and we were back in a tie for first place, both of us 6-4 with two games to play.

We traveled out to the West Coast for our final two games, and on Saturday afternoon, in miserable rainy weather, we shut out the San Francisco 49ers 13-0. Fuzzy and Em Tunnell and I went out and celebrated that night. We had some celebration; we spent about $1,000 congratulating ourselves. We woke up the next morning in a guy's apartment in Oakland, and we decided we'd stay there all day and watch the Colts play the Rams on television. We sent out for a loaf of bread and a few cans of tuna fish and a jar of mayonnaise, and out of the whole $1,000, that's all we spent on food. When the Rams beat the Colts, we clinched at least a tie for the Western Conference title.

The next day, while we were watching movies, getting ready for the Rams, I noticed that I was going blind in my left eye. My field of vision had changed. When I shut my right eye and moved a hand in front of my face, the hand disappeared about halfway across. With the right eye, I could see fine, more than a ninety-degree field of vision. I realized that I had a problem, but I didn't tell anyone. I'd mentioned something to the team doctor the week before, and he'd said that I had a piece of pigment knocked loose in my eye, nothing serious. So I didn't bother going back to him. I just went ahead and played the game, and we beat Los Angeles 35–21, and we were the champions of the Western Conference.

We went home to a hero's welcome in Green Bay —some ten thousand people came to the airport to cheer our plane in to a safe landing—and to start preparing for the NFL championship game against the Philadelphia Eagles. On Monday, our day off from practice, I went to see Dr. George Nadeau, an eye doctor in Green Bay. He examined my eye thoroughly and said, "Jerry, you've got a detached retina."

I'd never even heard of a detached retina before. I didn't have the slightest idea what it was. "We've got a championship game coming up in Philadelphia," I said. "Maybe we can get something done for the eye afterward."

"Jerry, this can make you blind," the doctor said. "It's very serious."

"So's this game," I said. "A lot of guys played their whole careers and never got to play in a championship game. I'm going to play this game. After that, we can do something."

I played the game, played the whole game, and I was a little nervous, mostly about getting hit in the head again and getting another concussion. My field of vision was cut down, but, as long as I kept both eyes open, not enough to hamper me. Sometime in the second quarter, I had to pull and trap Philadelphia's rookie outside linebacker, Maxie Baughan. It was a long trap, and we'd used the play a few times and made good yardage. When I pulled and started heading toward Baughan, he saw me coming and lowered his head and charged right at me. "Oh, no," I thought. I didn't have any choice. I just had to go right into him, head-to-head. We hit in the hole, and it was a hell of a collision. We both went flat on the ground, and Paul Hornung, carrying the ball, came through the hole and, as he went past, kicked me in the head.

I figured I was finished; I'd probably lost my sight in both eyes. I lifted myself up very slowly and looked around me, to the left, to the right, straight ahead. Everything looked all right. "Hey, I'm OK," I told myself. I stood up, and Maxie Baughan was still lying on the ground. He got up finally and hobbled over to the sidelines, holding his head. He got down on one knee and kept his hand against his head, and he stayed that way for three or four plays before he felt well enough to come back in.

We played a good game. I thought we deserved to win. But Paul got hurt in the third quarter, and the Eagles came from behind and beat us 17–13. The game ended with Jimmy Taylor, after taking a pass from Bart, getting tackled by old Chuck Bednarik of the Eagles just nine yards short of a touchdown.

I felt miserable about losing the game, about coming so close to the NFL championship and not getting it. From Philadelphia, I went right to a hospital in Madison, Wisconsin, to have my eye taken care of.

The best way to understand a detached retina, I suppose, is the way my doctor explained it to me. First, think of your eye as a basketball filled with water instead of air. Then think of the retina as the bladder inside the basketball. Detachment of the retina occurs when the retina gets torn, and the watery fluid runs through the tear and gets behind the retina. If you don't repair the tear, the fluid from the eye eventually causes total blindness. In 1960, there were two different ways of repairing a detached retina. The old method involved spending three weeks flat on your back, with your head sandbagged to prevent any movement; it involved some rather uncomplicated surgery, and the chance of success was about 50–50.

Dr. Mathew Davis of the University of Wisconsin had been using a new method of fixing detached retinas, a method developed in Boston that called for more radical surgery, but demanded a much shorter period of confinement. Most important, Dr. Davis had successfully repaired detached retinas in almost 90 per cent of his operations.

I went to the Davis and Duehr eye clinic in Madi-

son. For three days, they worked on making a minute-
ly detailed map of my eye. They dilated the eye,
beamed a bright light into it, and charted every blood
vessel, every indentation. Then, armed with a map
ten inches by ten inches, they operated.

They exposed the outer coat of the eye, the white
part, halfway back to the optic nerve and used an
electric needle to create scar tissue to seal the tear in
the retina. Then they sewed a piece of plastic into the
wall of the eye in order to push it against the retina
while the scar tissue formed. Then they bandaged
my eyes.

For three days, my eyes remained bandaged. I
couldn't see a thing, couldn't move my eyes. I had a
lot of time to think, to reflect, to worry about my sight.
It was a very difficult time to get through. If you want
to find out how much you enjoy your sight, wear a
blindfold for an hour, just one hour. The experience
probably should have scared me out of football. I
don't know why it didn't.

After three days, they took the bandages off my
right eye, my good eye. After another two days, they
took the bandages off my left eye. I had to remain in
the hospital a few more days, but on the eighth day
after the operation, I was released. On the ninth day,
I flew to Boise, Idaho, and the same afternoon I
played golf. I'll never forget that; I shot a 44 for
nine holes, a pretty good score for me, with my
wife's clubs.

Before I left the hospital, I asked Dr. Davis, "What
about football?"

He was a Packer fan, like almost everyone in Wisconsin. "I don't think you should play it any more,"
he said.

If I had any sense, I probably would have listened
to him. But I couldn't think of giving up football
not then, not when we had just come so close to
winning the championship, not when the team

seemed to be reaching a peak. "I'm going to play," I said to him, finally. "I've got to play."

Dr. Davis thought about it for a while, retraced the history of my eye with me, then offered me a little hope. "Well," he said, "the detachment doesn't seem to have hurt the vision at all. After it heals, the eye'll probably be stronger than it was before the detachment. If you re-detach it, I'm pretty sure we can fix it again. It may take one or two or three operations, but we'll do it. If that happens, of course, then there is absolutely no football."

"I want to try it," I said.

"It's up to you," Dr. Davis said. "You can try, but as a physician, I have to advise you not to."

I decided to play, and I guess Dr. Davis is pretty happy about it now. Ever since then, whenever he has a patient ask him, "If I have that operation, will my activities be restricted?" he says, "Well, Jerry Kramer had one, and he kept on playing pro football."

I spent most of the off-season brooding about the loss to Philadelphia. I was pleased by being named to the Associated Press All-Pro team, but I kept having dreams about the Eagle game, when I was asleep and when I was awake. We should have won the game. We had so many opportunities. I kept thinking about what I could have done differently, what we all could have done differently.

There had been some change in my thinking, my outlook, in the three years since I had arrived in Green Bay. Now, I couldn't believe defeat. I couldn't accept defeat. I had learned to think "win."

7

Toward Perfection

THE BALL WAS loose, rolling free near the line of scrimmage. I raced for the fumble, bent over, scooped up the ball on the dead run, and turned downfield. With a sudden burst of speed, I bolted past the line and past the linebackers. Only two defensive backs stood between me and the goal line. One came up fast, and I gave him a hip feint, stuck out my left arm in a classic straight-arm, caught him on the helmet, and shoved him to the ground. The final defender moved toward me, and I cut to the sidelines, swung sharply back to the middle for three steps, braked again, and reversed my direction once more. The defender tripped over his own feet in confusion. I trotted into the end zone, having covered seventy-eight yards on my touchdown run, happily flipped the football into the stands, turned and loped casually toward the sidelines. Then I woke up.

I know it isn't common knowledge, but I must

have scored ten or twenty touchdowns during my National Football League career, all of them in my sleep. In my recurring dream, I was always the hero, always the strongest, fastest, trickiest man on the field. I ran over opponents. I crushed them. I scored touchdowns. It was, for me, the ideal dream.

Vince Lombardi never told me whether he had any dreams or not, but I can imagine what his ideal dream would be. First, because he always takes the long-range view, his dream wouldn't cover one play or one game. His dream would cover, at the minimum, a full season, from the start of training camp to the end of the Super Bowl. In his dream, his team would win every exhibition, every regular-season game, every post-season game. They would win most games by a score of 35-0; he never believes in embarrassing an opponent by piling on the score. They would win the few crucial games by 42-0; he always believes in rising to special occasions. But the scores in his dreams would be secondary to the style. Every offensive lineman would execute each block crisply and cleanly. Each running back would find the proper hole each time, and would run harder the closer he got to the goal line. The quarterback would pass sparingly, but intelligently. The defensive players would tackle low and hard and fiercely. The kickoff team would trap the opposing runback man inside the 20-yard line every time, and the punting team, if Vince's team ever had to punt, would force a fair catch every time. Beyond any spectacular runs or spectacular passes, Lombardi would dream of a season without a single mental or physical error. He would dream of perfection, because Vincent Thomas Lombardi, above all else, is a perfectionist. Which is why, over the past decade, he has the finest record of any coach in professional football.

For Vince Lombardi, the first two years at Green

Bay were building years. By almost anyone else's standards, 1960 would be considered a year of accomplishment, but to Vince anything less than total victory, anything less than a National Football League title, was a building year. He needed those first two years to beat his system into us, to show us it would work, to give us confidence in him and in ourselves.

From then on, from 1961 through 1967, the peak years of the Lombardi era in Green Bay, he could concentrate on his real goal, on perfection. And in those seven years Vince Lombardi came as close to perfection as any coach, I suspect, will ever come. We won the National Football League championship five times, and in one of the two years we failed, we failed by only the slimmest of margins. In those seven years, we won 116 games and lost only 27, a percentage of .811. In post-season championship games alone, in games to determine conference, league, and Super Bowl titles, we were perfect. We won nine such games out of nine.

My only regret about those seven years is that injuries and illnesses forced me to miss large parts of three different seasons. In the other four seasons, I made All-Pro. The All-Pro nominations were flattering, but they were faint praise next to something Vince once said: "Jerry Kramer is the best guard in the league—some say the greatest in the history of the game." I know it's not very humble of me to repeat that, but I've got as much ego as anybody else. I needed all my ego to survive some of the other labels Vince used for me, such as "idiot," "jerk," "stupid," and "fat cow." I kind of like the last one the best; it's got a nice ring to it.

Each time Vince called me one of those less complimentary names, he had a reason, and the reason, basically, was always the same. I had made a mistake, mental or physical, and he felt I was too good to make mistakes. That's the way he felt about our whole team. He had created us, he had molded us, he had polished us, and every time we made a mistake, to his way of thinking, it meant that he had made a mistake, a teaching mistake. "I must be a lousy teacher," he'd say every time we violated one of his basic concepts. The only thing he hated worse than our mistakes were his own.

Of course, Vince didn't make too many mistakes in Green Bay, but I heard about one he made when he was coaching the offense for the New York Giants. The Giants built up a pretty good lead in an important game, and in the third or fourth quarter, Vince told his quarterback, Charlie Conerly, "Whatever you do, don't put the ball in the air. Don't pass. That's the law." Charlie had been having a good passing game, but when he switched to a running game, the offense fell apart. The Giants lost their momentum and lost the game. More than ten years later, Vince was still blaming himself for the defeat. "I never should have changed a winning style," he told Bill Heinz, the writer who's probably closer to Vince than any other. "It was stupid. I blew the game."

In 1961, for the second straight year, we lost our opening game. During the nine years of Lombardi, for some strange reason, we generally had trouble in our openers; of the nine games, we won only five. I wouldn't put anything past the man. Maybe he liked to see us lose the first game. Maybe he figured it would frighten us into playing better the rest of the year. The only game each season in which we had a worse record than in our first game was, for no apparent reason, the eighth game. We won our eighth game of the year only four times during Lombardi's coaching reign. Maybe he figured we needed a scare in the middle of the season, too.

We lost our eighth game in 1961, to Baltimore by a big score, but in between the first game and the eighth, we won six straight, all by eighteen points or more, including a 45–7 victory over the Colts. I thoroughly enjoyed five of those six victories; I could tell I was playing better than I ever had before.

Then, against the Minnesota Vikings in Minneapolis, I kicked off to start the game. It was a short kick and, because I was mad at myself for the weak kick, I tried to get downfield extra fast to hit the ball carrier. I got hit first. The wedge, the four big men shielding the ball carrier, smacked into me. I got hit from the side and from the back, and then the ball carrier trampled me. I couldn't stand up. The doctor and the trainer carried me off the field and put me on a stretcher. "You're OK," said Vince, feeling no pain at all. "You're OK. You'll be back and running in a couple of days." It was another one of Vince's rare mistakes. My season was over.

My left ankle hurt like hell, and when we got back to Green Bay that night, they X-rayed my ankle and found that I had separated two bones and severely stretched the ligaments. Still, they thought they'd be able to get me back in action before the end of the year. The doctors tried to pull the bones back together; they put a cast on the ankle, hoping that, without surgery, I would heal quickly. I stayed immobile for a week, wearing the cast, but when I left the hospital and tried to step on the foot, it hurt so bad I thought I'd die. So they put me back in the hospital and decided to operate and put a pin in the ankle. I thought it'd be a little, shiny, stainless steel pin, but I was wrong. They drilled a hole about two inches long, put a big bolt in it, put washers and nuts on either end, put the cast back and let it sit for another six weeks. By the time they took the cast off, it was too late to think about playing.

The funny thing—it's funny now, I guess—is that, at the same time I separated the bones in my ankle,

I broke my left leg and didn't even know it. At least, I think that's when I broke my leg.

I know I broke my leg sometime without realizing it because, during the 1963 season, I got kicked in the shins and I thought I might have a broken shinbone. I went to Jim Nellen, our orthopedic man, who X-rayed it and said, "No, it's all right. It's not broken. That other break of yours, you know, has healed up nicely."

"What break?" I said.

"Right here," he said, pointing just below my left knee. "Look on the X ray."

I suppose it could have happened anytime, but the only logical time was when I hurt the ankle. I was off the leg for a long time, giving the break a chance to heal.

(Incidentally, I'm not the only one who didn't notice all my injuries. When I hurt the shinbone, it happened very early, maybe the fourth or fifth play, in a game away from Green Bay. I didn't play almost the whole game. I got home that night with my shin bandaged up, limping like hell, and my wife met me at the airport. She didn't ask how I felt or anything. When we got to the house, I said, "Did you watch the game on television?" Barbara said, "Oh, yes. I watched every bit of it. Good game." I said, "Tell me about it," and she said, "I saw Paul miss an extra point, and Johnny got hurt, and Bart got hurt. Is Bart all right?" I nodded my head and started to get ready to go to bed. Barbara saw the big bandage all over my leg. "What happened?" she said. "Forget it," I said. "Go to sleep.")

If only my leg had been broken and not my ankle, I probably would have been able to play again in 1961. Lombardi has his own medical theories about broken bones in the leg. "The bone in the leg is not a weight-bearing bone," I heard him tell Lionel

Aldridge a few years later, when Lionel suffered a leg fracture. "It isn't necessary to the function of the leg. You've got two bones in there, and you only need one of them."

Vince never was one to cater to physical ailments, especially other people's. In that 1961 season, Dave Hanner had to undergo an emergency appendectomy a couple of days before we played San Francisco in our second game of the season. Hanner missed the San Francisco game, probably because he was still under anesthesia, then played a full game against the Chicago Bears the following week.

If our opening loss to Detroit frightened us into winning our next six games, then the loss to Baltimore frightened us into winning our next four games. The fourth victory in a row—20–17 over the New York Giants in Milwaukee—clinched the Western Conference title with two games still to play.

I felt like an outsider during the second half of the season, hobbling around the practice field and the stadium on crutches. It's strange how quickly you feel isolated, separated from the other guys. I went to every practice session and every game. I got sandwiches for the guys and I carried balls and I did all sorts of odd chores, but I was a hanger-on, not a participant. I was glad to see us destroy the Giants 37–0 in the NFL championship game, but I felt terribly frustrated, terribly useless. I celebrated after the game, but not as much as the other guys did. The game was played on Sunday, December 31, and on Tuesday, starting on my way home to Idaho, I drove past Fuzzy Thurston's house to say good-by to him. Fuzzy's wife, Sue, came to the door and said that Fuzzy hadn't gotten home yet from the New Year's Eve celebration. She wasn't particularly upset; he had been entertaining the whole world at the Northland Hotel in Green Bay, and he had earned his celebration. Fuzzy really had a hell of a year—

unanimous All-Pro, and the leading vote-getter on the team picked by the players—and I was happy for him, and a little bit jealous.

During the off-season, I walked and ran and lifted weights, trying to strengthen the ankle and the leg. The Achilles tendon had atrophied, after all that inactivity, and I had to stretch it back into condition. Most of the time, I worked out at the Y in Boise with Bob Dehlinger, a guy who'd been my teammate in college.

In June, when I felt like I was getting back in shape, Bob and I began fooling around with an old army surplus raft, big enough for fifteen people, floating around the Snake River and the Boise River. There was about twenty miles along the south fork of the Boise that was completely inaccessible by land except by one bridge. One day, we decided we'd start out early in the morning, float down to the bridge, and have a friend pick us up there around 6 P.M. We had a good trip down the river, shooting ducks and fishing. We had the raft loaded down with all our camping gear and hunting equipment. When we reached the bridge, about 5:30, the current was treacherously swift. Bob and I got out of the raft, holding it against the current, trying to walk toward the shore on sharp shale rock. Our rope holding the raft broke, and the damn thing swung around and started to drag us down the river. We almost drowned, trying to stop the raft, and by the time we got it under control, we were a mile and a half below the bridge. There was no way in the world to go back up the river. My foot was cut and swollen from the shale, and Bob and I had to haul the raft out of the water—it must have weighed 100 pounds with all the gear on it—then carry it 300 yards up a mountain to the road leading to the bridge. Because of the equipment, we had to make three trips, and it took us about three hours. When we finally got back to town, I went right to the hospital. I thought sure I'd broken the ankle again. I got it X-rayed and, to my amazement, it was still in one piece.

When I wasn't exercising or trying to drown myself in the Boise River, I was swearing to myself that I would have my finest season in 1962, that I would make up for not sharing so much of the excitement, and the glory, of 1961.

I didn't know it at the time, but Jim Nellen, the Packers' doctor, was just about convinced that I'd never be able to play again. He was afraid that the bones in my ankle wouldn't support my weight. He thought I'd probably separate them again. It wasn't until I'd been in training camp a week or two, knocking myself out, pushing myself as hard as I could, that I found out Jim had been so worried about me. But, by then, I'd shown him that my ankle would hold up.

In 1962, on the Green Bay Packers, everything came together. We came as close to perfection as any football team could. From the beginning of training camp, Lombardi kept impressing us with the challenge we faced. "Once you're on top," he said, "everybody wants to knock you off. This is the real test. This year you find out whether or not you're really champions."

We met the test. We reached the peak of our effectiveness as a team. We all had enough experience to get the shakes out of us. None of us was over the hill, or even thinking about it. We were strong. Lord, we were strong. The running backs were strong, the linemen were strong, every part of our game was strong. And, still, Vince rode us unmercifully, pouncing upon every slight imperfection. He had that gleam in his eye all year, the gleam that meant we'd better not do anything wrong, the gleam of a successful man seeking extra success.

Normally, I suppose it'd be kind of dull to recite

an entire lineup, but our 1962 lineup is worth reciting. There wasn't a dull spot in it. Start with the quarterback, Bart Starr. Bart was in his seventh season as a pro; he had just completed his first full season as a starting quarterback. His apprenticeship was over. He had knowledge, skill, confidence, everything, and, at twenty-eight, he was the ideal age for a quarterback. Bart completed more than 62 per cent of his passes in 1962; he was, statistically and in every other way, the best quarterback in football.

Jimmy Taylor, at fullback, was both the leading rusher and the leading scorer in the National Football League. Jimmy was a rock, a bull, incredibly strong and durable. He was twenty-six, an ideal age for a fullback, who requires a little less experience and a little more youthful abandon than a quarterback. The starting offensive line included Fuzzy and me at the guards, Forrest Gregg and Bob Skoronski at the tackles, all of us between twenty-six and twenty-nine, all of us except Gregg in our fifth professional season; Forrest was in his sixth year. The old man of the offense was Jim Ringo at center. Jim was thirty, in his tenth season, and there wasn't another center in the league even close to him. Our primary wide receivers were Boyd Dowler and Max McGee. Boyd was twenty-five, in his fourth season, and Max thirty, in his seventh season.

The defensive picture was pretty much the same. The interior line had Willie Davis and Bill Quinlan at the ends, Henry Jordan and Dave Hanner at the tackles, all with at least five years of competition behind them, all under thirty except Hanner, who was a very sturdy thirty-two. The linebackers were Dan Currie, Ray Nitschke, and Bill Forester; all had considerable experience and only Forester had hit thirty. The defensive backs were Hank Gremminger, Jess Whittenton, Willie Wood, and Herb Adderly, none older than twenty-eight. Adderly and Wood had the least experience of any of the regulars—Herb was in his second year, the only man in the lineup who hadn't started the year before, and Willie was in his third—but Wood led the NFL in interceptions, and Adderly made All-Pro. In fact, in 1962, fully half of our starting players, eleven of us, made one or more of the All-Pro teams. Six of us—Gregg, Currie, Forester, Ringo, Taylor, and me—were unanimous selections, named to every All-Pro team.

(Incidentally, of our twenty-two regulars in 1962, ten were still in the starting lineup six years later, which probably helps explain our decline in 1968.)

I deliberately haven't mentioned two of our starting players because they were special, each in his own way. One was Paul Hornung. In 1961, Paul had been named the Most Valuable Player in the National Football League and the outstanding performer in the championship game; he had led the league in scoring for the third straight year, even though he was in the army the last half of the season and missed most practices and two full games. Paul had scored 146 points in 1961; the only man in NFL history who'd ever scored more was Paul himself, in 1960, with 176 points.

Paul came out of the army just before we started training camp in 1962, and he was in miserable shape. He was overweight; he had no wind. Vince drove him and drove him and drove him, really punishing him. Paul was Vince's favorite, but Vince showed no favoritism; if anything, he leaned over backward to be doubly tough. He hated to see his boy out of condition. "You look like you're carrying a piano on your back!" Vince'd scream at Paul. "You look like you're carrying St. Norbert College on your back!" We all started calling Paul "St. Norbert." For ten straight days, we ended every practice session with a kickoff-return drill, and Paul had to return the kick, 100 yards at full speed. Vince damn near killed Paul, but by the opening game, he had whipped St. Norbert into shape.

We won the opener, for a change, beating Minnesota easily, and Paul had one of his greatest days. He scored three touchdowns, kicked two field goals, and kicked four extra points for a total of twenty-eight points. I helped him, with my blocking, on all three touchdowns, and I got off an especially good block on the third score, wiping out Jim Marshall, a defensive end, on a long pull. I was delighted with Paul's performance and delighted with my own. I felt I'd come back, and I felt Paul was ready for his best year.

But Paul had my kind of luck in 1962. In the fifth game, he got racked up, torn ligaments in his knee, and he hardly played the rest of the season. Tom Moore stepped in and took Paul's place and did an excellent job, but if we had one flaw in our perfect lineup, it was the absence of Paul. We missed his ability, and we missed his inspirational value. Paul's personality, his rare combination of nonchalance and determination, always lifted us. I took over his place-kicking job, and, while my kicking hasn't always been perfect, I did pretty well in 1962. I kicked thirty-eight extra points in thirty-nine attempts—Paul couldn't have done much better—and I kicked nine field goals in eleven attempts. Paul had kicked six field goals in nine attempts before he'd been hurt.

The other fellow I haven't mentioned was Ron Kramer, our tight end. Ron joined the Packers the year ahead of me, and he was probably the most publicized end ever to come out of college. Everyone knew Ron had tremendous ability, unlimited potential, but there was something wrong, something missing. He had a pretty good rookie year, then went into the service, and when he came out in 1959, we already had our starting lineup set. Ron didn't make a dent in it. He didn't catch a pass all season.

Gary Knafelc was our regular tight end in 1959 and 1960, and he was a good ballplayer, but he didn't have anywhere near the potential Ron had; for one thing, Gary weighed about thirty pounds less than Ron. I was friendly with Ron. We played golf together quite a bit, and our wives were close, and I liked him a lot. I couldn't figure out what was wrong. I couldn't figure out why he wasn't producing.

In 1960, in the middle of the season, we had an easy game against Dallas, and Ron got his first good chance of the year. He was awful. Bart threw one pass to him, a perfect pass, and it sailed right through his hands. Bart threw him another pass and it hit Ron in the helmet and bounced off. Bart threw to him a third time and the pass hit Ron in the shoulder pads, caromed up in the air, and was intercepted. The coaches took Ron out of the game. What the hell else could they do? He was hopeless.

At the beginning of the 1961 season, Lombardi took Ron aside and said, "You're either gonna play or get out of here. You're not going to sit on the bench." Lombardi hated to see talent going to waste. And, suddenly, Ron turned from an absolute mess into a super, super tight end. He was a fantastic blocker, really murderous, and once he caught the ball—he actually had great hands—he was almost impossible to drag down. One of my few pleasures in 1961, after my injury, was watching Ron develop. He reached a peak in the championship game against the Giants, catching four passes, two of them for touchdowns. Lombardi had worked his magic again, and he had done it in a different way again. With most of us, he just plain whipped us toward our full potential; with Bart, he used patience and understanding, quiet teaching; with Paul, he used confidence and faith; and with Ron, finally, he used gentle compliments, recognition of Ron's ability. Ron needed to be loved, like most of us, and once he realized that Lombardi loved him, that Lombardi needed him and wanted him, he became a great football player. He was one of the perfect cogs in our near-perfect 1962 machine.

Our record was as close to perfection as any National Football League team's has been since the play-off system began in 1933. No modern NFL team has ever gone through a complete season without a single defeat; the only teams that ever went undefeated during the regular season were the Chicago Bears of 1934 and the Chicago Bears of 1942, and both times the Bears lost the championship game. In 1962, including exhibitions and post-season games, we played twenty-one games; we won twenty of them.

We won six straight exhibitions and then we won our first ten games of the season. We won eleven of those sixteen games by more than two touchdowns, eight of them by more than three touchdowns. For the first time since I'd been a professional, we beat the Colts in Baltimore. Counting the 1961 championship game and the final game of the regular 1961 season, we won eighteen straight games. A lot of people called us the greatest team in the history of football, and most of us believed it.

Then we went into Detroit to play the Lions on Thanksgiving Day. Detroit had a strong team that year, an especially strong defensive team. They had two of the most important things in the world going for them on Thanksgiving Day—our extreme confidence and their extreme desire. I guess desire and motivation and incentive are all sort of interchangeable, but no matter which word you use, you can't overestimate its importance—in anything.

We'd beaten the Lions the first time we'd played them in 1962, but we'd just barely beaten them. They'd been winning 7–6 with just a couple of minutes to

play, when their quarterback, Milt Plum, had made
a pretty debatable call. He'd thrown a square-out pass,
a pass to the sidelines, a risky play, and Herb Adderly
had intercepted for us. We'd moved into scoring territory, and Paul had kicked his third field goal of the
day and we had won 9–7. The Lions, naturally, were
steaming and, on Thanksgiving Day, they were hungry for revenge, hungry to knock us off.

The Lions gambled. They anticipated. They
guessed. They blitzed. They red-dogged. Everything
they tried worked, and we looked absolutely foolish.
This is the sort of thing that happened: Bart would
call a screen pass, so Fuzzy and I would block Roger
Brown and Alex Karras for a short count, release them
quickly, then move out to the flank to form a guard
for the back who was getting the screen pass. We'd do
just what we were supposed to do, but one of their
defensive players would knock down the intended receiver, or tackle him, and Bart'd have no one to pass
to. There were millions and millions of people watching on nationwide television, and none of them would
realize that it was supposed to be a screen pass; all
they'd see would be Karras and Brown chasing after
Bart, ready to eat him up. All those millions of
viewers would wonder what the hell those supposedly
great Green Bay guards were doing, besides reading
their press clippings. The Lions caught Bart behind
the line of scrimmage eleven times, a new NFL record. They practically killed him, and they beat us 26–14.
That was the day that Fuzzy said he and I invented a
new block—the "lookout" block. We'd block, Fuzzy
said, and then we'd yell, "Look out, Bart."

We played the Los Angeles Rams in Milwaukee the
following week, and we came back strong and whipped them. I had a good game; I earned a blocking
award. Then we went out to the West Coast to play
San Francisco. Big Charlie Krueger of the 49ers beat
on me all day long, really gave me a physical pound-

ing. On one play, I got kicked in the ribs, a strong, painful kick. I came out of the game for just one play, then went back and finished. We won easily.

Lombardi kept us at Stanford, in Palo Alto, the following week, before our rematch with the Rams, and when I went out to practice Tuesday and Wednesday, I had a tremendous pain in my ribs. I didn't know it at the time, but I'd broken two ribs.

During the workout Wednesday, Ed Blaine, our reserve guard that year, was running plays, alternating with me and Fuzzy. Ed and I happened to be running together on one play, and he stumbled and fell, and I couldn't get around him or over him, so I pulled up. Vince started screaming. "Good guards, my tail!" he hollered. "We got the worst guards in the league!"

I was out there with my ribs all cracked up, killing me, and I was working as hard as I could, and Vince's remark really got to me. I hadn't even done anything wrong. I walked back to the huddle, and everyone bent over except me. I stood there, my hands on my hips, glaring at Vince, and he was looking away. I waited for something to happen. I could have quit right then if he had said something. Or I could have punched him. I was that mad. I had crazy thoughts running through my head, like, "If I punch him, it'll cost me a lot of money. I'll lose my game salary for the next game and I'll lose the championship money. What the hell am I gonna do?"

All this time, Bart was calling a play, and he broke the huddle, and everybody moved up to the line of scrimmage except me. I kept looking at Lombardi, and he still wouldn't look back. I didn't know what the hell to do. Finally, I sort of strolled up to the line of scrimmage and half bent over. I didn't get into my three-point stance. Bart called the signals, and everyone charged, and I didn't even move. I just stayed still. I walked back and stood behind the huddle, burnt to a crisp, absolutely disgusted. I let Fuzzy and

Ed Blaine run the next few plays. Then practice ended, and I was still steaming. Vince played it just right, as always. He came over and patted me on the back and messed up my hair and said, "I'm sorry, I didn't mean that. I wasn't talking about you, you know that."

We won our final game in Los Angeles, came home and found out my ribs were broken, shrugged it off— "I guess they don't hurt any more," Lombardi said— and got ready for the NFL championship game. The Giants had won the Eastern Conference title again. We played them in New York, but it was real Green Bay weather, miserably cold, the temperature in the teens, the playing field hard as concrete, and the wind blowing about thirty-five miles an hour. It was a crazy wind, too, the way it often is in stadiums. The wind'd blow one way at ground level and the opposite way twenty yards up in the air, one way at one end of the field and the opposite way at the other end. Yankee Stadium scared the hell out of me, anyway, with its traditions and everything else. I'd only played there once before, in 1959, and we'd been beaten. I guess I was still a country boy, impressed by the big city and the big stadium.

In the first quarter, we had a scoring drive stall deep inside the Giants' territory, and I tried a field goal from the 26-yard line. I didn't even try to figure the wind. I was still kind of awed by the idea of kicking in such a big game in such a big place. Generally, I never look at the other team when I'm kicking—I just look at the ground and try to draw an imaginary line between the spot where the quarterback's going to place the ball and the spot where I'm aiming—but this time I looked across the line of scrimmage and I saw Dick Modzelewski and Sam Huff and Rosey Grier and Andy Robustelli and all the great New York Giants, and I had a quick thought about them, about how good they were. But then I kept my head down and kicked, and when I looked up, the ball had already passed the goal posts. It was off to the side. I cursed under my breath, and I turned around, and the referee had his arms up in the air signaling that the kick was good. "What the hell's he doing?" I said to Bart, who had held the ball for me, and Bart said, "Shut up and get off the field."

I thought sure I'd missed the kick. Later on, somebody told me that, in the official's estimation, the ball had passed between the uprights and then the wind had pushed it outside. I was pretty happy. We were ahead 3–0.

I missed my next field goal attempt, then made one, then missed another. On both my misses, I tried to allow for the wind, and the ball sailed straight, straight outside the goal posts. On the second kick I made, just like the first one, I aimed straight for the middle and the wind almost carried it off target.

In the fourth quarter, right near the end of the game, we had a 13–7 lead and we set up another field goal attempt at the 30-yard line. "If you make it," I told myself, "it's all over. We've got the game won."

I kept my head down, kicked right down the middle and the ball stayed straight all the way. As I lifted my head, I caught a view of the sidelines and I saw Lombardi with a clenched fist in the air, a victory sign. And then Fuzzy jumped on me and all the guys jumped on me and started beating me on the back. It was a great moment—we won 16–7—and, in every way, a great game for me. I'd recovered a fumble, and I'd knocked my man, Modzelewski, around quite a bit. On our one touchdown, I got in a real good lick.

From the New York 7-yard line, Bart called a 37, a play designed basically to go outside our right tackle, off our right end. Modzelewski read the play. Something in Jimmy Taylor's stance warned Mo that the play was going outside, and he took a step in that direction to stop the play. I charged after Mo, made good contact, and drove him farther outside, and Jimmy Taylor adjusted, cut back to the middle—running for daylight—and went for the touchdown. The play was supposed to go through the "seven" hole, and it actually went through the "zero" hole, the center's spot.

I thought I'd played a hell of a game, and, apparently, my teammates thought so, too. They voted me the game ball, the only game ball I ever actually earned during my eleven years with Green Bay. (I did get another game ball—after we beat Cleveland in 1964—but that was because the guys thought I was about to die. I didn't play in the Cleveland game. I was on my way to the Mayo Clinic.) But I didn't get the sports car that SPORT Magazine presents each year to the outstanding performer in the championship game. Ray Nitschke got the car. He played a tremendous game, blocking a pass and recovering two fumbles and tackling all over the field, but I was still a little disappointed.

It was a very punishing game physically, and I remember, on the plane going home, we were all still so cold we wore our overcoats. Jimmy Taylor and Paul Hornung and Max McGee and Jess Whittenton and I played cards in the lounge in the back of the plane, and whenever Jimmy'd reach for a card, his arm would shake, still chilled and trembling two or three hours after the game.

I planned on a real big celebration that night. It was probably the best game I ever played under huge pressure, and I felt I'd earned a big night. It didn't work out. My wife and I went to the King's X, a restaurant owned by Jess Whittenton, and when we walked in, the people who'd watched the game on television had already been celebrating for hours. They were all in a high state of excitement and intoxication. A woman spotted me and yelled, "Hey," and grabbed me by the arm. My elbows and my knees were both raw from the ground and the body contact at Yankee Stadium; every bit of skin had been rubbed off. When the woman grabbed me, she touched a raw elbow. "Get your hands off me and leave me alone," I snapped.

"Can I have your autograph?" she said.

"No," I said. "You can't."

I think that's the only time I ever refused to sign an autograph. There have been occasions when I haven't had enough time to sign a bunch of autographs, but that was the only time I flatly refused a request.

I was so aggravated with that lady, and then some guy, who'd been drinking since dawn, turned around and shouted, "Hey, there's one of them." He started pawing me and pulling me around, and I knocked his hands off me, turned to my wife and said, "C'mon, let's get out of here."

We left and went to the Italian Village and I had spaghetti and meatballs and a big glass of milk and went home and went to bed. That was my big celebration.

It wasn't until the next day that I was really able to savor the taste of that game, what we had done, what I had done. It was so sweet. I had come all the way back from my injury. I felt like I was on a cloud. I loved everyone in the world. I was even sorry I'd turned down that lady's request for an autograph. I wanted to go outside and talk to everybody and smile and laugh, I felt so good. I had that same glow after some of our later victories, our Super Bowl victories, and after *Instant Replay* became a best seller. There is something about success that makes all the hard work that went into it seem worthwhile. The feeling may not last long. It may fade in a week or in a day or in an hour, but while it's there, it's a beautiful feeling.

Two weeks later, I played, for the first time, in the Pro Bowl game in Los Angeles. I remember, after the 1959 season, I'd watched the Pro Bowl on television with my father, and he'd said, "How come you're not playing?"

"It takes a while to make it," I said. "I need about three years' experience. I'll be there next year."

I got to the Pro Bowl two years behind schedule—I would've made it after the 1961 season, I think, if I hadn't been hurt—but it was still a big thrill. It meant that I was part of the elite, the best of the pros. I played in the Pro Bowl three times, but the first time was the best. I had fun. I made a lasting friendship with Merlin Olsen of the Rams; it was nice to have him on my side, instead of facing me. It was even nice to have Alex Karras on my side.

About ten days after the Pro Bowl, on January 23, 1963, they held a JFK Night—a Jerry "Football" Kramer Night—in Sandpoint. There must've been two or three hundred people there, and half of them were relatives. My mother and father were there, and my brother and sisters and aunts and uncles and grandparents, and it was a lovely night. Charlie Stidwell, my junior high principal, was there, and Cotton Barlow, my high school coach. Skip Stahley, my college coach, announced that the University of Idaho was retiring my uniform, that no one else would ever wear 64 at Idaho. I got a tremendous charge from the evening, and, again, everything seemed worth-while, all the aches and injuries forgotten. I couldn't help thinking about how lucky I was, how few people had ever come out of Sandpoint, or any town like Sandpoint, and gone to college and become a professional football player and become a championship football player. The odds had to be so high against me when I started. I've always believed that you make your own luck, but I did get a lot of breaks, a lot of help from other people. I was glad that I had a chance in Sandpoint, on my twenty-seventh birthday, to thank some of the people who had helped me.

When we returned to Green Bay for the 1963 season, training camp just didn't seem the same. It wasn't. Paul Hornung wasn't there. Paul had been suspended from the National Football League for betting on football games. (Alex Karras had been suspended too.) We missed Paul. We missed his spirit. The previous year, when he had been out with injuries, even his physical presence, limping and giggling, had helped. But in 1963 we saw him only on rare occasions, when he stopped by to watch us play.

Vince missed Paul too. Coach had been hurt by the fact that Paul hadn't confided in him, hadn't let him know that he was in trouble with the NFL office, but still Vince missed Paul. More than ever before, which is saying a lot, Lombardi wanted to win in 1963. No team had ever won three NFL championship games in a row, and Vince wanted us to be the first. We played well, but it just wasn't our turn. The Chicago Bears were destined to win.

We played the Bears the opening game of the year in Green Bay, and they had beat us 10–3. We should have known something then. Every bounce, every call, every break went their way. Yet we weren't too upset. We'd lost our openers in 1960 and 1961 and had managed to win the Western Conference title each year.

After the opening defeat we won eight straight games, all of them by more than a touchdown. In seven consecutive games, we scored thirty or more points, something the Green Bay Packers never did before in the NFL and have never done since. Our blocking triggered a powerful running game. Jimmy Taylor and Tom Moore, replacing Paul again, were both among the leading ground-gainers in the league. And, in all modesty, our place-kicking game was unbelievably good. In our first eight games alone, I kicked fifteen field goals out of twenty-five attempts.

I also kicked twenty-six extra points. I was leading the NFL in scoring, and the league office put out a press release talking about all the field goal records I could break. For instance, in the history of the Packers, no man had ever kicked even seventeen field goals in a full season. I didn't, either. I saw that press release and I read all the stories in the papers, and I got the lump. I choked up.

In the last six games, I kicked only one field goal out of nine attempts. I had gotten so anxious I was looking up too soon, trying to see the ball pass between the uprights, just like a golfer lifting his head to admire his shot. All I saw was the ball sailing off to the left or to the right or under the crossbar. I didn't find out what I was doing wrong until the final game of the season. We finished the year in San Francisco, and at the end of the game, after I'd missed three attempts, Tommy Davis, the 49ers' place-kicker, walked up to me and said, "Jerry, you're lifting your head." It was a little late by then. I managed to finish with ninety-one points, which placed me fourth in the NFL in scoring.

The Bears ended our winning streak after eight games, which really stunned me because we were as charged up for that game as we ever were. We knew we had to beat them and we were ready, we were up. I remember thinking that we were going to massacre them, maybe 73–0 or something like that. Then we went out and Bart threw a pass and it hit one of their linemen in the helmet and bounced up in the air. Doug Atkins, their big defensive end, caught it and lumbered about twenty yards down the sideline to set up a field goal. Things like that kept on happening, and Chicago beat us 26–7.

Even though we remained in contention until the final day of the season, it was really Chicago's year. After the season, Doug Atkins told me about a game they had played against Pittsburgh late in the year.

In the closing minutes, the Bears and the Steelers were tied. Chicago had the ball deep in its own territory, inside the 10-yard line, and their quarterback threw a pass out in the flat. A Pittsburgh linebacker stood squarely in front of the ball. All he had to do was grab the ball and walk into the end zone and Pittsburgh would win. The pass hit the linebacker in the chest, bounced out of his arms, and fell to the ground. Doug was sitting on the bench at the time, and he turned to his teammates and said, "Boys, you might as well spend your money 'cause there ain't no way in the world we can lose this thing now."

I helped the Chicago cause a little when, two weeks after we played them, I missed an extra point against Detroit. My old buddy, Wayne Walker, kicked two field goals and an extra point to give the Lions a 13–13 tie. At the time, I was afraid that missed point—it was blocked—might be very costly. But as the season turned out, it didn't make any significant difference. We finished the year with a record of 11-2-1; a record of 12-2 still wouldn't have been enough to match Chicago's 11-1-2.

The extra point was blocked by Detroit's John Gordy on a real freaky play. Gordy was up on the line and he was supposed to grab one of our blockers and throw him, and then Wayne Walker, from his linebacker position, was supposed to shoot through the hole Gordy had created and try to block the kick. Gordy reached for our man, grabbed him, then lost his grip and slipped. At the same time, Wayne came charging into the line, full speed, slammed into Gordy's back, and sort of squirted him into our backfield. "I just threw my hand up in self-protection," Gordy told me later, "and I hit the ball." It was that kind of year for us.

After the Lions game, after I'd missed that damn extra point, I felt miserable. When we got back to Green Bay that night, I told my wife we were going to dinner at The Ribs, thirty-five miles out of town, because I didn't want to see anyone I knew. We walked into The Ribs, and the first person I spotted was Jim Nellen, the team doctor. Then I saw the assistant coaches. Then I saw Vince. It was his birthday party, and it just about killed me. I'd driven thirty-five miles to be under his beautiful gaze.

We played in the post-season runner-up game in Miami, and we couldn't get very excited about it. Lombardi said it was "a hinky-dinky game played by hinky-dinky teams in a hinky-dinky town," and most of the players agreed with him. We didn't train too hard, and Vince, for once, didn't seem to care. We had no curfew New Year's Eve, the Tuesday before the game, and when we practiced on Wednesday, the whole huddle just reeked of alcohol. It was foul. Bart Starr kept pretending he was getting dizzy from the smell. He called one play, "OK, red right, and winos hook—on two." We beat the Cleveland Browns—I guess they had a few parties, too—and as soon as the game was over, I flew to Los Angeles to join the Western Conference team in the Pro Bowl game.

The next morning, on the bus going to practice, George Halas, the Bears' coach who was handling the Western team, handed me a playbook. I opened it up and the first play I saw was a 49, the Green Bay sweep, utilizing the same blocking we used. The reciprocal play—opposite runner to the opposite side—was a 28, the same as ours.

I thumbed through the book, and I saw that Halas had given me the entire Green Bay offense, play for play, number for number, right down to our formations, the red and the brown.

I looked up, a little surprised, and Halas' assistants were grinning, anticipating my reaction. "We were going to put in the blue formation, too, Jerry," one of them said, "but we didn't think we had enough time. We knew you boys from Green Bay would be late coming in here and we didn't want you to be behind everyone else."

The Chicago coaching staff wasn't just being considerate. They'd learned a lesson. The year before, Lombardi had coached in the Pro Bowl, using the Green Bay system, and Bill George, Chicago's middle linebacker, had picked up quite a bit of information about our offense. He learned and retained a lot of our plays, a lot of our audibles. Then, when we played the Bears, they'd set up a gap defense, and Bart'd come up to the line of scrimmage, see the defense and call an audible, an automatic signal changing our play to a 41-trap. As soon as Bill George would hear Bart say "Forty-one," he'd yell, "Watch the trap. Watch the trap. Here they come up the middle." Halas wasn't about to let the same thing happen to him, so he put in the Green Bay offense, instead of the Chicago offense. Nobody liked to give away little tips during the Pro Bowl.

One of the first people I saw on the practice field in Los Angeles was a rather skinny guy wearing old-fashioned, metal-rimmed glasses. He didn't look at all like a professional football player. He looked more like somebody's kid brother. I couldn't believe it when we were introduced. He was Raymond Berry, the great end from the Baltimore Colts.

I'd never met Berry before, and I'd never seen him closeup, but I'd heard so much about what a perfectionist he was, how hard he worked, how he was totally dedicated to football. I found out that everything I'd heard was true. Raymond Berry was living proof that desire could turn a player with less than ordinary physical equipment into a brilliant star.

All the other guys on the Western Conference team would come out to practice in T shirts—we weren't scrimmaging—but Ray Berry would come out in full uniform, hip pads, thigh pads, shoulder pads, helmet, everything. He'd go through each workout completely geared up, to simulate game conditions. Before everyone else got on the field, he'd find someone to throw him passes next to a grandstand or next to a screen so he could get the feeling of catching the ball close to a defender. He tested sunglasses, attached to his helmet, to see if they would help him in the California sun. Jimmy Taylor kept kidding Raymond and calling him a welder. "Hey, get that welder out of here," Jimmy yelled.

Berry had a bad back, a short leg, and miserable eyesight, but he had a total commitment to success. He burned to be the best and, Lord, how he worked at it. I found out that before every game, an hour or so before anyone else came out on the field, Raymond would walk the entire field, end zone to end zone, sideline to sideline, checking for wet spots, hard spots, slopes, any tiny detail that might give him an edge over a defensive man. He was supposed to be one of the all-time great students of game movies; he'd take them home every night and watch them for hours, analyzing every defensive back's moves. Nothing that Raymond Berry could possibly do himself was ever left to chance.

I admired Raymond tremendously, and I learned from him. Now, when I have to do anything that I'm not perfectly equipped to do—public speaking, for instance—I think of Berry and I'm reminded to prepare myself thoroughly. I want to know my audience, know the mood of the occasion, know all the circumstances surrounding my speech, know anything that'll help my delivery be more effective. I'm studying the field, just like he did, and I'm working on my moves and on my timing. And I've become a pretty good speaker; the audience always seems to laugh at the right time. Maybe they're afraid that, if they don't, I'll hit them.

In the summer of 1964, I lived in Green Bay and made all that money working for the tire company in

Madison. In July, as always, I reported to training camp, and in August, my intestinal problems began.

During the exhibition season, I began running a low-grade fever and getting stomach pains. The harder I worked on the field, the more severe the pains. Any time I took a deep breath I was in agony. The team physician looked me over and said that I probaby just had gas on the stomach, that my wife had been cooking too many beans. Then, at the end of August, we went to Dallas to play the Cowboys and I really felt miserable. My weight had dropped about fifteen pounds to 240. My temperature was up around 101 or 101.5. I could tell I was weaker than I should be. The team physician examined me again, detected some swelling in one of the abdominal muscles, and treated me with cortisone and procaine. The procaine, at least, killed part of the pain.

The following week, we played our final exhibition game, in Cleveland against the Browns, as part of their traditional exhibition doubleheader. By then, I was getting chest pains as well as stomach pains and my weight had slipped to 237. Before the game, Bill Quinlan, who'd been traded to Detroit, came to see me in my hotel room; the Lions were playing in the other half of the doubleheader. "God, you're skinny," Quinlan said. "You look terrible."

"No," I lied. "I'm in great shape. I'm feeling fine." I wasn't going to tell him that I was sick.

I went out for the game, and Frank Parker of the Browns really threw me around. He just ran over me, stamping on me, trampling me, and I tried to hang on for dear life. I held him. I even tackled him. I did anything I could to stop him, but I still wasn't very effective.

All through the next week, while we were preparing for our opening game, my pains kept getting worse. On Thursday night, we had a poker game at my house, and I love to play poker about as much as anything in the world. My pains were so bad I had to quit the game after an hour and go upstairs and lie down. I couldn't breathe properly; the pains had spread to my back too. I didn't do a thing in practice Friday and Saturday, but on Sunday, against the Bears, the defending NFL champions, I played the whole game. I was shot up with cortisone and procaine again, and I guess I didn't do too badly. We won the game.

By Monday, I was in agony again. I practiced Tuesday, then rested Wednesday, practiced Thursday, rested Friday and Saturday. I was still running a fever, still wracked by intestinal pains. Yet I wanted to play against the Baltimore Colts on Sunday. The doctors pumped me full of procaine and wrapped my ribs in tape, like I had broken ribs, and I went out and played the first quarter. I was a mess, an absolute mess. Sometime in the first half, I felt so sick I couldn't breathe, so I came out of the game, kneeled near our bench, and tried to catch my breath. "What is it?" Bill Austin, our line coach, asked me. "What's the matter?"

"I'll be all right," I said. "Just let me get my breath and I'll go back in."

"No," Bill said.

"Just give me a minute," I said. "Let me go back in."

"You're not playing," Austin said. "Sit down."

I didn't play any more that game—or any more that season—and, afterward, I went to the hospital, and a doctor examined me and found a lump just under my breastbone. He was almost certain that he had detected a cancerous growth. I thought, too, that I had cancer. My doctor, a general practitioner, suggested that he bring in a young surgeon to take a look at me, a new fellow in Green Bay, a surgeon named Bob Brault. "The hell with any Bob Brault," I said. "I want an experienced doctor. I don't want anybody learning on me."

Bob Brault came in, and that was one of the best things that ever happened to me. Bob Brault is a genius. Eventually, he found out what the trouble was. Eventually, he saved my life.

A few days after the Baltimore game, Bob Brault operated on me and discovered a tumor about the size of a grapefruit growing on my liver. It was full of pus. This was the same area where I'd been getting the procaine injections, and it isn't too far-fetched to think that a needle could have punctured the tumor and allowed the pus to escape into the intestinal tract. Peritonitis might have set in, and I could have been dead.

Dr. Brault diagnosed my ailment as actinomycosis bovis, which is a fungus. I was sitting in Dr. Brault's office one day, and I opened a medical text and read that actinomycosis in the intestinal tract is uniformly fatal. I was ready to give up until Doc told me that the medical book was out of date. He cut the tumor open and drained it and packed it and tried to let it heal from the inside out.

I was in the hospital about two weeks with the wound healing, and Fuzzy Thurston came in to visit me. Bob Brault walked into the room while Fuzzy was there, and Bob said, "Fuzzy, I've got to change his bandages. Do you want to leave the room?"

"What do you mean—leave the room?" Fuzzy said. "Hell, no. I'll watch."

Doc Brault took off the bandages and started peeling the gauze out of the wound. He used two pairs of scissors. With one pair, he'd pick up the loose end of the gauze and pull it out, and with the other pair he'd snip off the gauze near the wound. Fuzzy took one look at the gash in my belly, and he damn near passed out. He turned white and staggered over to the window and started staring out. Fuzzy didn't ask to watch again.

When I finally got out of the hospital, I started attending practice sessions, but I couldn't do anything except run errands. I felt miserable, just like an outsider again, not a part of the team at all. One morning I went duck hunting with Doc Brault and we got stuck out in the water, almost blown into Lake Michigan, and I showed up at practice two hours late. Normally, whether I was healthy or sick, I would have been hit with a big fine. "Where in hell have you been?" Vince demanded.

"Seeing my doctor," I said. I never could lie to Vince.

"From now on," Lombardi said, "make your appointments after practice."

While I was suffering, the team was in bad shape, too. We won three and lost two—to Baltimore and Minnesota—by one point each. Paul Hornung had been reinstated, but he was still rusty from his year off. His kicking, in particular, was giving him trouble. He missed an extra point in each of those one-point defeats. Then we played the Colts in Baltimore, and Paul missed four field goals, and we lost by three points.

The next week, I went out on the field after practice was over and started place-kicking. I kicked the hell out of the ball. I moved back to forty-five, fifty yards from the goal posts, and I used a kicking tee, and I put kick after kick right between the uprights. Dad Braisher, the equipment manager, happened to see me out the window and he called the coaches and they watched, too.

"What were you doing?" Lombardi said, when I came in.

"I can kick," I said. "I can help. I can do something."

"OK," said Lombardi. "You're kicking this week."

When I saw Bob Brault, I told him I was going to

kick, and he said, "No! Absolutely not." He meant it, too.

I had to call Lombardi and tell him that I couldn't kick, and when I told him, I started to cry. I felt so damn bad.

We split our next four games, and with four games to play, our record was 5-5. Baltimore was 9-1, and we were finished. I went out one night and got good and drunk, and the next day, my temperature shot up to 103, my intestinal pains intensified, and I went back in the hospital. Dr. Brault found a new lump growing down inside my groin near the abdomen. My wife and I decided I ought to go to the Mayo Clinic, and after I watched the team beat Cleveland, after I received the game ball from my teammates, I took off for Minnesota for the resection of my large intestine, for all the horror of the colostomy. Many of my teammates thought they'd never see me again.

I guess I disappointed them. Six months later, thanks to Bob Brault's brilliance in searching for and finding the splinters that had stayed inside me for twelve years, I felt like I wanted to play football again.

Around the end of June, coach Lombardi spoke at a banquet in Spokane, Washington, and, naturally, the people out there asked him whether I'd be playing in 1965. "No," Vince said. "It doesn't look like Kramer will ever be able to play any more."

I heard about Vince's remark, and when he got back to town, I went to his office. "What's this about?" I said.

"I don't think you're going to be able to play," he said.

"I'm planning on playing."

"Well, if you can, it's wonderful," Vince said, "but I just can't count on you. I don't think you can play."

I can't blame him too much. I showed up for training camp weighing maybe 225 or 230 pounds, short of wind, and feeling weak. About a week after practice began, I developed a bubble and a slight infection in the area below my breastbone where I'd had the hernia repaired. I went to the doctor and he made a slit about two inches long and half an inch deep to let the area heal from the inside out. I went to practice for a few weeks that way, with a hole in my stomach. I didn't practice too hard. Lombardi kept me out of contact work and told me to stay with the defensive unit. "Go over there where you won't bother anybody," he said.

Vince didn't even want me to do calisthenics, but I argued with him. "I've got to get in shape," I said. Finally, we worked out a compromise. Donny Chandler and I would stand in the back row during calisthenics, and we'd alternate doing the exercises. Donny wasn't supposed to do too much because he was a kicker—he'd just come to us from the Giants to salvage our kicking game—and he didn't want to pull a muscle or get his legs all tightened up. It was a perfect deal. If everyone else did twenty sit-ups, I'd do five and then Donny'd do five, and then I'd do five, and then he'd do five.

Early in August, when I got my weight up close to 240 and I felt a little stronger, Vince put me back with the offense. The day of our first exhibition game, against the New York Giants in Green Bay, I went over to the stadium and signed my 1965 contract. Vince had assured me that I'd be paid for the season even if I couldn't play, but the fact that he was actually giving me a contract made me feel good. "Just fill in a figure," I said, "and I'll sign it." I wasn't about to try to hit Vince for a pay raise.

That night, the Giants didn't give us any trouble, and Vince put me into the game. I'll never forget the roar of the crowd when I ran onto the field. It seemed like everybody in the stadium stood up and started to cheer. It was a beautiful feeling to hear something like that. I knew it wasn't for the quarterback. It wasn't for the running back. It wasn't for any of the other guys. It was for me.

I felt a chill running up and down my back. I hadn't heard an ovation like that for me personally since I was in high school and I was playing in a basketball game against a kid who was about six foot eight. I stepped away from him and went up with a right-handed hook shot, shooting with the claw hand less than a year after the hunting accident, and the shot went in and the gymnasium exploded. There were a lot more people, of course, in Lambeau Stadium in Green Bay.

Lombardi let me stay in for three or four plays. The next week, he let me play half a quarter against the Bears in Milwaukee. My strength and my timing and my agility gradually returned, but I didn't start any of the exhibition games and I didn't start at the beginning of the season.

In the fifth game of the regular season, my good friend Alex Karras got my starting job back for me. I'd been playing a little each game, but a young fellow named Dan Grimm was starting at right guard. Dan had played a real good game against Alex the previous year, when I was out, but Alex had been hurting that game and he was looking for revenge.

The week before the Lions game, I watched Alex very closely in the movies, studying him in case I got a chance to play. I wasn't going to tell Danny Grimm anything; I was just going to let him suffer. Along about Thursday, I started feeling guilty and I took Dan aside and said, "Look, let me tell you what I think about Alex. He's got a real quick move to the outside. It's his first move generally. Then he'll hop, then he'll move again and try to beat you. He's got to be close to you to beat you. He's got to be right on top of you."

"Yeah," said Danny.

"If he's not close to you," I went on, "he can't throw you. So what I did against him—and I found it pretty effective—was that when he made his first move, I'd move back about two feet. He'd have to start all over again. It'd throw him off. He'd have to start his whole plan again."

"Yeah," said Danny.

"Sometimes," I said, "you can attack him right in the middle of his move, but you better make damn sure you stick him or he'll get away."

Fuzzy Thurston and Forrest Gregg, who'd both played opposite Alex, were listening, and they both said, "Jerry's right."

"Nope," Danny said. "It may be all right for Jerry, but I don't think it'll work for me. That's not my style."

"Beautiful," I said to myself. "Beautiful."

Danny went out and played his own style and got his ass kicked. Alex just chewed him up and spit him out in the first half. Alex tore off Danny's helmet two or three times and got to Bart three or four times. We were trailing at half time, something like 21–3. I moved in at right guard for the second half, and we came back and won the game 31–21.

Vince came up to me and Fuzzy after the game—he'd been benching Fuzzy once in a while—and he said, "You're my guards. Yeah, yeah, my guards. I'll never make that mistake again." A week or two later, Vince had us both back on the bench. But we started the last five games of the season, and it was a dramatic year.

After opening the season with six straight victories, we lost three of our next five games to bring our record to 8-3. Baltimore was 9-1-1, a game and a half in front of us. Then Chicago upset Baltimore, and Johnny Unitas got hurt, knocked out of action for the rest of the season. We went into Baltimore the following week, Paul Hornung scored five touchdowns—following Fuzzy and me, of course—and we won that game and took over first place, half a game ahead of the Colts.

In the final game of the year, Baltimore, using halfback Tom Matte at quarterback, beat the Los Angeles Rams, and we got tied by San Francisco, forcing us into a playoff for the Western Conference title.

The playoff was in Green Bay, and it was a bruising physical game. We were tied 10–10 at the end of regulation play. Donny Chandler had tied it up with a field goal just like the one I'd kicked against the Giants in the 1963 championship game. Donny was afraid he'd missed the mark, but the referee signaled the kick was good. After almost fourteen minutes of sudden-death overtime, Chandler kicked another field goal—there was no question about this one—and we had a 13–10 victory.

For me, the championship game against the Cleveland Browns provided a tremendously satisfying ending to a satisfying season. In a way, I'd worked harder than I'd ever had to work before. In a normal season, my aches and pains after a game would disappear by Tuesday or Wednesday. But in 1965, I never felt right until Thursday early in the year and until Friday late in the year. For the championship game, I ached right up till the morning of the game.

I played a good game against the Browns. I brush-blocked two men on Paul's touchdown run, the one that turned a tight 13–12 contest into an easy 23–12 victory. I didn't feel too much joy or elation; the championship was nothing new. But I did feel satisfaction.

The next two years, of course, were deeply satisfying. I shook off all signs of my injuries and my sicknesses and I made All-Pro both years. I started every game in 1966 and every game in 1967, and with Lombardi prodding us and whipping us and screaming at us with the same fury he had shown right from the beginning, we won the Western Conference championship both years, the National Football League championship both years, and the first two Super Bowl games.

The third straight National Football League championship was by far the highlight for the team and for me personally. It was our goal, our target, our dream, the one thing all of us wanted to accomplish before we completed our football careers. It placed us up on a pinnacle that all future teams can shoot at. It soothed, temporarily, the burning within Vince Lombardi. It wasn't perfect, but it would do until perfection came along.

For me, the championship game, the dramatic game-winning block on Jethro Pugh of the Dallas Cowboys, meant a sudden rise from anonymity, an opportunity for nationwide television exposure that taught millions of people who I was, that gave me, finally, my own identity in professional football. Sure, people still stop me and say, "You're Ron Kramer, aren't you, the guy who played end for Michigan?" but not as many as used to.

The burning within me was soothed too. I had achieved all the goals I had set for myself in professional football. I had accomplished everything I wanted to accomplish, except one thing. Only one dream failed to come true. I never did score a touchdown.

8

A New Life

IT ISN'T EASY to give up professional football. It isn't easy to surrender a way of life that has been both profitable and pleasant. I remember the agony friends of mine went through when they dropped out of football. When I think that I'll never play another game, I think, especially, of Don Chandler.

Donny and I were teammates for three years, roommates for one, and we became very close friends. Donny's a bright guy, a sensitive guy, and I value his friendship. After the 1967 season, when he began to talk of retiring, I didn't take him very seriously. I figured he could keep place-kicking for another five years.

Then, in the spring of 1968, I visited Donny at his home in Tulsa to discuss a business deal. At the end of my stay, he drove me to the airport. His little boy, Bret, came with us; Bret was seven years old, and he'd been practicing place-kicking since he was three.

Donny and Bret walked with me to the gate to my plane, and as I started to say good-by, Donny tried to say something. He had difficulty getting the words out. Maybe it was my imagination, but I thought he had a lump in his throat. Donny is not normally an emotional guy, but I could tell he felt very emotional. "Well, pal," he finally managed to say, "this is it."

Suddenly, I realized he meant it. He was giving up football. I shook his hand and watched him turn around and walk away. He put his arm around his boy's shoulders, and, in a way, the boy symbolized to me what would replace football in Donny's life. I stared at them, disappearing down the corridor of the airport, Donny's arm still shielding his son, the two of them fading in the distance like the final shot of some corny movie. I felt a little emptiness, as if I were losing a part of my life.

Donny must have felt the same emptiness even more strongly. When he got home, his wife Pat later told my wife, he lay down on the sofa and, for about two hours, with his hands cupped behind his head, he just looked at the ceiling. I'm sure that all the years ran through his mind, the eight championship games he played in with the Giants and the Packers, the dozens of field goals and the hundreds of extra points he kicked, each memory permanently preserved. I get misty-eyed just thinking about it.

Thinking about Don sets me thinking about similar incidents. I remember when Gary Knafelc was traded to San Francisco. Gary had been a Packer for nine years and he felt a strong attachment to the team. When Lombardi told him he'd been traded, he asked Vince not to tell anyone else. Gary practiced that morning and went through the entire session without saying a word to anyone. Then we broke for lunch, and in the afternoon, we practiced again. Gary and Bart Starr were very close, and they'd developed a set ritual. Whenever Bart started working with the receivers, Gary was always the first in line; he always caught the first pass.

The afternoon of the day Gary was traded, all the receivers lined up, and someone yelled, "Knafelc! Where the hell's Knafelc?" A couple of the guys started hollering for Knafelc, and, all of a sudden, they realized Gary wasn't there. It didn't take too long for everyone to realize what had happened, and, again, there was a strange feeling of emptiness. When we got back to the dorm after practice, Gary had moved out all his belongings. He had left for San Francisco. He couldn't face the guys.

My decision to retire from professional football is the most important decision of my life up till now. I know it's not quite so drastic as a doctor giving up private practice to go into research, or a lawyer deciding to join the Peace Corps, or anything like that, but, still, to me it's got to be very significant. It means I'm changing my whole way of life. I'll no longer be playing a silly game every Sunday afternoon. But I can't help thinking that maybe, instead, I'll be playing a different silly game every day. I'll be playing the money game, the business game.

In a sense, even though I've been playing the business game seriously for the past four or five years, I'll be a rookie again. I'll be starting all over. It's sort of like moving from college football to professional football. You're doing the same thing, basically, only you're doing it on a bigger scale for bigger stakes.

I was awfully naïve when I first got into the business world. I remember when we started in the archery business, with the American Archery Company, my partners and I went to a bank to borrow $150,000. I'd never dealt with a sum like that before. I still get excited about large sums. When I sign a big check, for $10,000 or $20,000, I can feel the adrenalin flowing, just like after a good block.

My partners and I had to sit down with the president of the bank and the vice-president and a few other people, all of us gathered around a big conference table. Up till then, the only bank people I'd dealt with were tellers. The president of the bank said, "Well, you want to borrow $150,000, and I don't see anything wrong with that." He said that he did want to know how we were going to pay him back. Everybody was just sitting there, and my partners weren't saying anything, so I rushed in and stated the obvious. "We're going to make bows and arrows," I said, "and sell them for a little more than it costs us to make them, and pay you back out of the profits."

The bank president was a nice man. He didn't laugh. He just nodded and began talking about accounting procedures and cash flow, and I thought to myself, "What the hell is cash flow?" But I knew enough then to keep my mouth shut.

Obviously, I wasn't very knowledgeable about business, but I liked the excitement of it, just as I liked the excitement of football. Competition is the main thing in both fields, and if you don't enjoy competition—clean, hard competition, I mean—you're not going to be a huge success in either. You can still be a perfectly fine person. I know lots of people who don't thrive on competition, who are more passive, and they're good people. Sometimes I envy them their lack of competitiveness; they save themselves a great deal of disappointment. But they're the way they are, and I'm the way I am—I certainly can't judge who's better off—and I've found, in meeting all kinds of people, that the ones who get to the top, as lawyers or doctors or singers or writers, are the ones who have a strong competitive instinct. I'm like that. I want to win, at poker, golf, and everything else.

I'm not trying to put everything in sports terms. I've heard people apply the clichés of sports to every other phase of life, and I know how ridiculous it can sound. You hear someone say, "I really scored on this deal," or, "I couldn't get to first base on that deal," or, "I've got my back to the goal line," or something like that, and sometimes you want to laugh. They get carried away. But I don't think I'd be reaching too far to apply my experiences in football to almost everything else I do. After all, I've invested a big chunk of my life in football; it's still what I know best. In *Instant Replay*, I compared Lombardi and the Packers with Shakespeare's Petruchio and Kate, and I didn't feel self-conscious about that. By the same token, I don't feel self-conscious about comparing football with business.

I'm going to try to apply the same principles to being a professional businessman that I applied to being a professional football player. I'll start off with a bit of an edge. It's not like going into the College All-Star game wondering what I'm doing on the same field with the All-Americans. I've already had enough experience in the business game to know that I can make it as long as I work hard at it. And I've got the desire, the motivation. I want to prove myself. I want to show I'm not just a big football player who can shake a few hands and smile at everybody and get patted on the back for being able to say "Hello."

I'm not fooling myself. I know that a lot of the business success I've enjoyed so far has come because I played professional football, because people wanted to associate with a pro football player, wanted to help him and advise him, and perhaps share some of his occupational glamor. I know damn well that the glamor of pro football is going to wear off me very quickly, and then I'm going to have to make it on my own.

I hope and I think that I know myself, and that's one of the basic requirements for success. I know my own strengths and, even more important, I know my own weaknesses. I'm not an accounting genius. I'm no expert on the law or on the stock market or on much of anything else except trap-blocking. But I am smart enough to look for the right people to advise me in the areas where I'm ignorant, to seek out their opinions, and not to accept them blindly, but to consider them and weigh them and see if they make sense to me.

Beyond not deluding myself about what I can do and what I can't do, I want to accumulate as much knowledge as possible about each field of business I enter. Take the diving business, for instance. I went into it practically blind, but I lived out on the rig for a few days to get a feel of the business. Since then, I've learned a lot more. I've put on the scuba gear myself and gone down and watched the divers at work, watched them laying pipe and capping wells. I'm never going to be a full-time diver, but when I go to people from oil companies and try to persuade them to give me their diving contracts, I want to be able to discuss the subject intelligently. I try to learn as much as I can about my opposition, too, what other diving companies offer in the way of services, what they charge, what their strengths and weaknesses are. It's all just a matter of solid preparation, something I'd want to do in any field. Suppose I go into television work on an extensive basis. I'm going to study successful announcers, in sports and out of sports, and try to learn the tricks of the profession.

Thorough preparation is largely hard work, and hard work, pretty obviously, is an essential part of success. "The harder you work," Vince Lombardi used to say, "the harder it is to give up." I'll swear by the truth of Vince's slogan. Late in many seasons, when I faced critical situations in critical games, when I might have been tempted to give up or to take it easy, I remembered how hard I'd worked preparing for the season or the game and I doubled my efforts.

And that's another thing I'll carry over into business—extra effort, or, as Vince called it, second effort, the willingness to extend yourself, under pressure, beyond normal limits. Incidentally, I'm going to try to keep myself in good physical condition, too. If you're not in shape, second effort—and sometimes first—comes hard.

If there's one principle, above all others, that I've taken from football and that I intend to follow in business, it is: Think "Win." That's the absolute key, as far as I'm concerned. It means forgetting about second place, forgetting about coming close, and forgetting about almost; it means thinking constantly about winning and thinking that you can win and thinking that you will win.

I don't want to be pretty good or fairly good or a little above average in anything I do. I want to be the best. Realistically, I know that I'm not always going to be the best, but that won't stop me from seeking to be the best, from doing everything within my power to be the best. I'm in the real estate field, and I want to build more and bigger apartment houses and office buildings than anyone else. I'm in the restaurant franchising business, and I want my chain to be the most popular and the most efficient. I want to see every sportsman in the country using my bows and my arrows, and I want to see everybody who needs diving services hiring my company to do the job.

I've finished second a couple of times, and I know it isn't much fun. It can be profitable to finish second, highly profitable, but there just isn't the same enjoyment, the same satisfaction, the same exhilaration. As a businessman, I'm going to be looking for enjoyment and satisfaction and exhilaration. I'm going to be looking for financial rewards, too, but that's not primary. I'm not trying to suggest that I don't care about money. I do. I believe what someone once said to me: "Money isn't important, but it's the only way to keep score."

When it comes to keeping score, I've got to admit that I'm not the most meticulous person in the world. My checking account seems to be overdrawn most of the time. My banker, Gene Sladky, is always calling me up and saying something like, "Jerry, you're ninety-three hundred dollars overdrawn."

"Well, lend me ten thousand dollars," I'll say.

"You were seventy-four hundred dollars overdrawn two weeks ago," Gene'll say, "and you borrowed eight thousand dollars. Never saw anybody go through money the way you do. Better make it fifteen thousand dollars this time."

It's not that I'm really deep in debt. It's just that I try to keep my money working for me all the time. I don't like to leave too much of it sitting in the bank.

I've set a specific financial goal for myself. In the next three years, I'd like to bring my total assets up to $1 million. I figure if I'm going to keep score, it might as well be a nice round number, one that I won't have any trouble remembering.

I've got a pretty good start toward my goal. I'm working at so many different things right now. Early in 1969, Urban Henry and I sold the Packer Diving Company, but we've both still got management contracts. I've been making speeches and filming TV commercials and collecting royalties from the sales of *Instant Replay*. I own stock in the parent corporation of the Red Rams, the franchising group I'm involved with, and I also own part of four individual restaurants. I own about 18 to 20 per cent of the archery company and an equal share of a subsidiary corporation that makes hunting films. Don Chandler and I own a 92-unit apartment house and have an option on a piece of property to start a 108-unit building.

In addition, a friend of mine who's in the oil

business, Obie Shaw, has offered me an opportunity to get into that area, and Rod McKuen and I have talked about going into the discount record field, and Dale Robertson, the actor, and I have discussed the cattle business. Throw in the fact that I expect to be working on football telecasts and that I own two houses in Idaho, a house and a farm in Green Bay, and a condominium in Florida, and you can see that I'm pretty diversified. You might even say I'm spread a little thin.

I do worry about jumping into too many different things. I fear that it might all get out of control, that it might become just a vast, vague empire, almost entirely out of my hands. I like the idea of being a quarterback at business.

I have other worries about playing the money game. I worry about the loneliness of success. I'm still excited and stimulated by business, but I worry that I might become too wrapped up in the rat race, that I might reach the point where I'm making money only for the sake of making money, where I'm not really enjoying myself.

I'm awfully tempted at times to drop out of the rat race. Maybe now. Maybe two or three years from now. And, of course, maybe never; maybe it's just wishful thinking, maybe it's just a dream that'll always elude me.

Yet it is appealing, the thought of retreating to a placid life, perhaps the quiet, pleasant life of Sandpoint, Idaho. I suppose Sandpoint exists in my mind only the way it was fifteen or twenty years ago, but I still have my dreams about it.

I remember that people lived very comfortably in Sandpoint on relatively little money. An income of $10,000 a year put a man among the wealthy class. He could have a boat and golf clubs and guns and fishing gear, and he could live a healthful life, applying no pressure to anyone, feeling no pressure from anyone. Even though the cost of living has gone up everywhere, I'm positive that I could live well in Sandpoint just on the income from the money I've got now.

I can see myself in Sandpoint. I can see myself playing golf during the warm months, skiing during the cold months, hunting during most of the year. I can see myself out on Lake Pend Oreille, drifting in a rowboat, fishing with my father. Dad has one big goal in life now, to find that thirty-eight-pound rainbow trout that'll set a new world record, and he spends hour after hour on the lake, trolling and waiting and hoping. It must be nice to have such a specific ambition, to know exactly what you're looking for in life. I'd love to join Dad in his search. I'd love to sit out there, peaceful and relaxed, feeling the sun and the clean air, waiting for the granddaddy of all trout to strike.

I could do it. I've got everything I'd ever need to live the good life in Sandpoint. I've got enough sporting equipment to stock two stores. I've bought myself so many guns, so many fishing reels, so many sets of hunting and fishing and skiing clothes. Sometimes I suspect that the reason I've bought all these things is just in case my business ventures collapse, just in case everything suddenly falls apart, I'll still have the things I really need to enjoy myself.

Now I realize there's a conflict in what I'm saying. On one hand, I'm talking about dedicating myself to success in business, and on the other, I'm talking about withdrawing from the money game and simply relaxing. It's a real conflict, an honest conflict. I am torn. I'm not the sort of person who's easily satisfied with himself—I'm often very dissatisfied with things I do—yet, at the same time, I seem to enjoy most of life at the moment. I can be so easily pleased by life, by a funny joke, by a good friend, by a sweet song, by a doe prancing across a field, and still down deep, something gnaws at me. Something says I should be doing more, or doing things differently. Maybe the difficulty is that I'm able to get satisfaction out of everything, and out of nothing. I always like what I'm doing, and regret what I'm not doing. I don't suppose there's any easy answer to that sort of dilemma, but I do think about it a lot.

One of the reasons I'm tempted to lessen my pace, I'm sure, is that I'd like to spend more time with my children. I've never had enough time for them; I've been running in recent years, on the field and off. I like my children and I love them, and I want to give them a zest, an enthusiasm, for the basic pleasures of life. I'm selfish, I guess. I want them to share and like what I like.

I guess that's why, in 1968, I purchased and stocked a big, old farm outside Green Bay. I looked for three or four months before I found a place I liked, a perfectly secluded place. To get there, you follow a highway, then a blacktop road, then a county road, then a gravel road. My gate's at the end of the gravel road. I've got a hundred acres, and forty or fifty acres in the back border a twenty-square-mile national forest. There's nobody behind me and nobody within half a mile on either side. I've got trees and paths and a spring-fed fish pond, maybe forty yards long and twenty yards wide, with a good, cold bottom. I'm stocking it mostly with trout. I've got three pups, a great Dane, a St. Bernard, and an Irish wolfhound; I let the kids think they were choosing them, but I guess, actually, I picked what I liked. I suppose because I'm big I've got a psychological thing for big dogs. I've got two Shetland ponies and I'm getting a third, so that each of my children, Diane and Tony and Danny, will have his own pony.

One day after the 1968 season, Susan Jordan, Henry's daughter, and Danny, both of them four years old, got on one of the Shetland ponies together.

Diane or Tony offered to lead the pony, but Danny said he didn't want anyone leading. He kicked the pony to get it running, and the pony bounded away, and Susan and Danny both tumbled into a big, fluffy pile of snow. They started giggling, and pretty soon they were both laughing so hard they couldn't stand up. They'd get up and stagger and break into hysterics laughing and fall down again. I got the biggest charge out of the scene, until I saw the pony going over the hill, heading for the back forty. I went out and chased him, wading through snow drifts up to my stomach, and it took me two and a half hours to bring that little Shetland pony back.

The kids seem to love the farm as much as I do. One day early in 1969, I was in Chicago, on business for the Red Rams, and I promised Danny I'd be home in time to take him out to the farm that night. The meeting dragged on and on and didn't break up till almost midnight. I didn't want to disappoint Danny, so I persuaded a friend to fly me up to Green Bay in his plane. I reached the house around 3:30 A.M., and Danny woke up and said, "We going to the farm, Dad?"

"Guess I will," I said.

"I better go with you," Danny said. "I don't want you to be alone."

He went to his mother and said, "Mom, I'm going to the farm with Dad. You got somebody to sit ya?"

Barbara told Danny that she'd be all right with Diane and Tony, so a little after four in the morning, Danny and I drove out to the farm. Once we got there, he decided that he wanted to watch television. I was too tired to argue, so I let him watch the test patterns for about half an hour. He didn't seem bored; I guess he's a real lineman's son.

I really enjoy the children, fishing with them and riding with them and just sitting around and reading to them. I even bought two huge contour chairs that fit next to each other so that all four of us can sit together while I read out loud. I hope that, no matter how hard I decide to work or what I choose to do, I'll be able to spend enough time with them, together and individually. They're a pleasure.

Just to make things a little more confusing, besides choosing between the business life and the Sandpoint life, there's still another direction that tempts me. I keep thinking about getting involved in some form of public service, about putting all my energies into government or politics. From time to time, I think that I'd like to give up all my businesses or put them in somebody else's hands, go back to college, earn my bachelor's degree, and then maybe get a law degree and pursue a career in public service. I think I might be able to accomplish some good. That's one of the things that gnaws at me, whether I'm accomplishing anything of value. So many people have done so much for me—back to Uncle Bob in Sunday school, Charlie Stidwell at Farmin Junior High, my coaches, my doctors, the friends I've made—and I'd like to be able to do things for other people. It sounds corny, but I'd like to lift people, help them do what they can do, help them enjoy their lives. I've never been terribly attracted to party politics—I tend to judge people as individuals, not by labels—but sometimes I think about running for public office. I don't have any experience at that, but I do like meeting people and talking to them, and I guess that's a big part of the game.

Early in 1968, I found myself intrigued by politics generally and by Robert F. Kennedy particularly. I liked what he was trying to do. I liked the way he could communicate with the young people and with the minorities. I liked the fact that he was a guy who didn't have to do anything for a living, but that he had chosen to devote himself to public service. When he was killed, I felt as wounded as most Americans. I felt a good deal of pain and some bitterness.

Although I offered to help in the re-election campaign of Senator Gaylord Nelson in Wisconsin, after Senator Kennedy's death, I didn't get too involved in the campaigns of any of the other presidential candidates. I did end up attending a sportsmen's dinner for Richard Nixon, and I introduced the other football players present. It was pretty exciting, especially when I found that the guests were paying $500 a plate. I'm surprised I managed to get through the introductions without stuttering. Later on, I attended the inaugural ceremonies in Washington, and I could feel the thrill of politics. It's a big game, bigger than any I've played yet.

I'll confess that my mind turns toward Washington a lot, and not always to the White House. I think about the other man there. I think about Vince Lombardi. In May 1969, not long after I'd made my decision to retire, I spoke at a sales meeting in Florida, and my speech accompanied a showing of "Second Effort," an inspirational film starring Vincent Thomas Lombardi. I'd seen the movie before, but when the screen showed Lombardi and a salesman standing in a completely empty stadium, the wind blowing across the field, a cold and lonesome scene, I started thinking about all the moments I'd spent in that stadium and all the people I'd known there and how difficult it was going to be to leave it all behind. I weighed 270 pounds that day, but the next week, I watched my diet and I got down to 260, only a few pounds above my 1968 playing weight.

As I watched the movie, I wondered whether I would have quit if Vince had still been coaching. I had some strange thoughts. What the hell would I say if, after I announced my retirement, Vince traded for me, gave Green Bay a third-round or fourth-round draft choice for the right to deal with me? Suppose Vince got me in a corner and told me that he needed me and asked me to come out of retirement to play for him. What would I tell him? I just didn't know what my answer would be. Despite everything else I've said, despite all my arguments with myself, I'd love to play for that man again. I'd love to play for him in a whole new situation, to grow again with him.

I think he's going to do well in Washington. I thoroughly believe that the emotional aspect of football is by far the most important, and I don't think I've ever seen anyone who understands the emotional aspect as well as Vince Lombardi.

Months before training camp opened in 1969, Vince had begun his campaign of psychological warfare. From what I read in the newspapers, he had already made Sonny Jurgensen, Washington's great quarterback, a true believer in the Lombardi system. Between Sonny's arm and Vince's head, I think the Redskins are going to win a lot of football games in the next few years. It would be fun to be part of it.

For days after that meeting in Florida, I thought about the possibility of playing for Vince. I thought, too, about the new pains that were creeping into my back and my neck. For eleven years, I'd been sticking my head into 280-pound defensive tackles, and there isn't much difference between hitting some of those guys and hitting a wall. I guess all those collisions wore down my neck and my back, and the pains are catching up with me. I thought, very specifically, about Alan Page, the young bull from Minnesota who'd weighed 300 pounds and been stronger than hell in 1968, his second professional season. He was probably just starting to reach his peak, just starting to approach his full strength. Alan Page is the best argument I know for retirement. I might not be able to say no to Vince, but if I were trapped in a room with Lombardi and Page and both of them told me I ought to play another year, I wouldn't listen to them.

I'm retired. I'm through. I'm tempted by politics and I'm tempted by Sandpoint and I'm tempted by Vince Lombardi, but I suspect, strongly, I'm moving headfirst into business. I'm going to wear suits, not shoulder pads. I'm going to wear ties, not cleats. I'm going to sip martinis at noon, not Gatorade. I'm never going to hit Alex Karras again. I'm never going to get hit by Alex Karras again. "LOOK OUT, BART!" Good-by football.

Jerry Kramer's Medical History

AGE 3—Dropped axe and fell on it, cutting chin and throat. Stitches.

AGE 7—Fell out of tree. Cut arm open. Stitches.

AGE 14—Caught T shirt in turning screw of lathe. Ripped out fist-sized chunk of right side. Stitches.

AGE 15—Accidentally shot right arm and side with double-barrel 10-gauge shotgun. Wound required four operations, skin grafts, and plastic surgery over the next few years.

AGE 17—Ran into sharp board while chasing calf in pasture. Seven-and-one-half inch long, three-quarter inch thick splinter penetrated groin and lodged in large muscle near spine. Major operation.

AGE 18—Brain concussion sustained in football game.

AGE 19—Operation for suspected chipped vertebra in neck.

AGE 20—Brain concussion sustained in football game.

AGE 23—Brain concussion and detached retina of left eye sustained in game against Los Angeles Rams in 1960. Operation to correct detached retina delayed until after season.

AGE 24—Two bones in left ankle separated and ligaments severely strained during game with Minnesota Vikings in 1961. Left shin also broken but not discovered until 1963.

AGE 25—Two ribs broken during game with San Francisco 49ers in 1962.

AGE 28—Operation for tumor on liver. Emergency colostomy. Postoperative pneumonia. Six-and-one-half hour operation in lower left abdominal area during which four slivers of wood (that had been lodged for eleven years) were removed. Operation to close colostomy. Operation for hernia near breastbone.

AGE 32—Right thumb broken in game against Atlanta Falcons. Ligaments of right knee stretched in game against Detroit Lions. Nerves in shoulder pinched in later game.

ABOUT THE AUTHOR

GERALD LOUIS KRAMER is, at thirty-three, a product of Sandpoint (Idaho) High School, the University of Idaho, and the Green Bay Packers. Five times an All-National Football League lineman, his first book, *Instant Replay*, was his diary of the 1967 professional football season.

ABOUT THE EDITOR

DICK SCHAAP, former syndicated columnist, former city editor of the New York HERALD TRIBUNE, and former senior editor of NEWSWEEK, collaborated with Mr. Kramer on *Instant Replay*. He is also the author of *R. F. K.*, *Turned On*, *An Illustrated History of the Olympics*, *Paul Hornung*, and *Mickey Mantle*.

Wait 'til you see what *else* we've got in store for you!

Send for your FREE catalog of Bantam Bestsellers today!

This money-saving catalog lists hundreds of bestsellers originally priced from $3.75 to $15.00—yours now in Bantam paperback editions for just 50¢ to $1.95! Here is a great opportunity to read the good books you've missed and add to your private library at huge savings! The catalog is FREE! So don't delay—send for yours today!